"Jeff Haanen invites both an elevated ima[...] a practical theology for work and the human condition. Whether you are an educator or an executive, the invitation is to renew your mind on work, engage a deep calling, and spend more days fully alive. I wish I had read this twenty years ago!"

Mike Sharrow, CEO of C12 Business Forums

"In this thoughtful, inspiring, and practical book, we are reminded that the perilous Sunday-to-Monday gap is not only about doing work differently but also about becoming a different kind of person. The matter of who we are becoming is of the greatest importance. We love, serve, and lead others in the world out of the overflow of our inner world. For anyone who desires to experience a more seamless life of integral faith in their Monday world, Jeff Haanen is a wise and seasoned guide. *Working from the Inside Out* is a welcome and needed voice in the broader faith and work movement. I highly recommend it."

Tom Nelson, president of Made to Flourish and author of *The Economics of Neighborly Love*

"*Working from the Inside Out* provides a much-needed foundation and framework for the integration of spiritual and cultural renewal. It calls us to a vision of costly discipleship through pursuing spiritual vibrancy, sacrificial relationships, and good work for the betterment of society. This book leaves the reader inspired to live for the kingdom in every square inch of creation. Followers of Jesus—read this book."

Billy Waters, lead pastor of Wellspring Anglican Church

"Jeff Haanen is one of the foremost thought leaders of this generation on the topic of faith and work. In *Working from the Inside Out*, Jeff provides anecdotal and prescriptive insights that will inspire and move you to action. Jeff's wisdom and perception are profound in helping readers bridge the sacred/secular divide. This book helps you understand how your work can serve as the most valuable tool Christians have to make a difference in the world. However, we must change internally before we can change the external world."

David Stidham, vice president of business affairs and general counsel for *The Chosen*

"*Working from the Inside Out* is a book I will recommend to a broad range of people without caveats. It's accessible and profound at the same time, as Jeff Haanen puts flesh on theory, pairing his insights about spiritual formation and our need for wholeness with real-life narratives. It's also theologically astute while keeping a foot on the ground—as Haanen is clear-eyed about the varied realities and challenges that different kinds of workers face. It moved me and reminded me of my own longings for greater wholeness. I'm confident it will do the same for you."

Matt Rusten, executive director of Made to Flourish

"In Jeff Haanen's latest work, the reorienting message of the gospel is placed at the center of what it means to live out one's vocation in daily work. Based on insights from one of the nation's leading thought leaders in the faith and work movement, this book will be a great resource for anyone who wants a flourishing, purpose-driven life."

D. Michael Lindsay, president of Taylor University and author of *Hinge Moments: Making the Most of Life's Transitions*

"You don't need this book—if you love your job, live a balanced life, can't wait to get up in the morning, and feel content in your relationships with people and God. If not, consider this collection of deep wisdom from an expert in the crucial, but often ignored, intersection of faith and work."

Philip Yancey, author of *Fearfully and Wonderfully* and *Where the Light Fell*

"In *Working from the Inside Out,* Jeff Haanen takes on what takes us on. Navigating who we are becoming as we navigate the complexities of how we work is a unique challenge in the cultural moment where we find ourselves. For followers of Jesus, reckoning with our work offers us the great opportunity to discover our Creator's vision for a healthy relationship with work."

Chris Horst, chief advancement officer at HOPE International and coauthor of *Mission Drift*

"Jeff Haanen has long been a pacesetter in the faith and work movement, and here he's doing it again. Through a deft mix of theological and personal reflection, he shows that the integration of the gospel and our work first takes place inside us before it makes a difference in the world. His focus on the inward journey, not just activity and productivity, models wisdom for Christians who want to bring together their public and private worlds."

Hunter Beaumont, lead pastor of Fellowship Denver Church

"I can't wait to give this book to some important people in my life! As the title suggests, Jeff Haanen's most valuable contribution is his focus on our inner spiritual life and the promise that a life attuned to the hope, love, and grace of the gospel changes us. Work is a crucible; it forms and shapes us—for better or for worse. Jeff's five guiding principles (seek deep spiritual health, think theologically, embrace relationships, create good work, and serve others), developed and tested during his decade with Denver Institute for Faith & Work, offer a way toward work forming us 'for better.' Read with friends; take this journey together."

Katherine Leary Alsdorf, founding director of Redeemer Presbyterian Church's Center for Faith and Work

Working from the Inside Out

A Brief Guide to Inner Work That Transforms Our Outer World

Jeff Haanen

An imprint of InterVarsity Press
Downers Grove, Illinois

InterVarsity Press
P.O. Box 1400 | Downers Grove, IL 60515-1426
ivpress.com | email@ivpress.com

InterVarsity Press® is the publishing division of InterVarsity Christian Fellowship/USA®. For more information, visit intervarsity.org.

Published in association with the literary agency of Wolgemuth & Wilson.

The publisher cannot verify the accuracy or functionality of website URLs used in this book beyond the date of publication.

Cover design: David Fassett
Interior design: Jeanna Wiggins
Cover image: © mycola / Getty Images

ISBN 978-1-5140-0331-2 (print) | ISBN 978-1-5140-0332-9 (digital)

Printed in the United States of America ♾

Library of Congress Cataloging-in-Publication Data
A catalog record for this book is available from the Library of Congress.

30 29 28 27 26 25 24 23 | 13 12 11 10 9 8 7 6 5 4 3 2 1

FOR KELLY

Thank you for your

grace and your friendship

in my journey of becoming.

The highest reward for a person's toil is not what they get for it, but what they become by it.

JOHN RUSKIN

Contents

PART 1

Disintegration

1

Fragmented Lives, Fractured Culture

Are you tired? Worn out? Burned out on religion? Come to me.
Get away with me and you'll recover your life. I'll show you how
to take a real rest. Walk with me and work with me—watch
how I do it. Learn the unforced rhythms of grace. I won't lay
anything heavy or ill-fitting on you. Keep company with me
and you'll learn to live freely and lightly.

MATTHEW 11:28-30 MSG

We sat on the sideline of a windswept soccer field. It was between games at the Wichita Fall Invitational in Kansas. Parents watched their sons eat mandarin oranges and bagels between games, surrounded by cleats, soccer socks, and cheers in the distance.

I sat next to Amy, the mother of three sons, and talked life, work, and family as the fall sun shone on our faces. She turned the conversation to her husband, Brent, and their early marriage and career. "We moved to Idaho and followed them out there," Amy said, referring to a couple who had mentored Brent and Amy during their time as Young Life leaders after college. "In only weeks, the business—and our mentors—fell apart. We had just bought a house, and now we were jobless. What were we supposed to do?" Pain settled in just months after the wedding day.

As Amy recounted the rocky start to Brent's career, the conversation quickly became more honest. "Work has been such a struggle for him," she said about her husband's occupational odyssey. Holding various midlevel business roles, Brent now works for a wholesale alcoholic beverage distributor. "Years ago, Brent fell into a deep depression. It was pretty scary. I don't think he likes what his work is doing to him," she said, explaining the false persona he's had to put on during tough business negotiations.

This weighty story about Brent caught me by surprise. Brent is vibrant, always positive, in great shape, and exudes energy.

Later that evening at our hotel, I asked Brent directly about his day job. "I help people make more money from booze," he said with a defeated laugh. "I only send one-sentence work emails."

I learned that Brent's early aspirations for an up-and-to-the-right business career had been squeezed out like a tube of toothpaste, and meaning that had escaped him in his career now became transferred to hobbies, coaching, and family. Work paid the bills and happened to be close to his home. But nothing more. His wife said he usually avoided the subject of work, as he felt a tinge of shame he hadn't been more of a "success."

LONGING FOR MEANING

Work is where we spend most of our adult lives. The average adult will spend ninety thousand hours, or a third of their adult lives, at the job. And yet work—not just for Brent—is a shared struggle for nearly all of us.

One summer, we at Denver Institute for Faith & Work, the educational organization I founded, studied how people *felt* about their work. We did surveys and dozens of first-hand interviews. People spoke of being proud of their work and seeing the value in what they do. But they also shared their heartaches: "I feel like no matter what I do it won't make a difference. I wish I could make an impact." "I feel isolated from those who share my Christian values in my workplace." "I feel intense pressure to perform and meet demands." "I feel like nobody cares about my values as long as I perform." "I feel like my faith community doesn't understand my working life." "I feel like my boss doesn't recognize what I contribute around here." "I feel rushed, busied, and overwhelmed by the responsibilities of life. I can't do one more thing."

We sense that work must be more than a paycheck, a way to make an imprint on the world around us. Christians in particular yearn to connect heart, mind, and work to meaningful contribution to the world. And yet, doing so is often fraught with difficulty and setbacks. Even success can breed disillusionment.

Owen Hill's early career was meteoric. He attended the Air Force Academy and then graduated with a PhD in policy analysis from the Pardee RAND Graduate School in Santa Monica, California. He was elected to the Colorado State Senate at age thirty. Having cosponsored several successful bills in Colorado, he decided to "wager it all" six years later and run for US Congress. He largely self-funded his campaign for the US House of Representatives—and lost. After losing to a long-standing incumbent, he felt growing tension around broad Republican support for personality rather than policy, so Owen decided to leave politics altogether.

Nearly penniless and jobless after a decade in politics, Owen reflected one evening over dinner about his work, "What was it really for? Did I accomplish anything that will last?" A nagging sense of emptiness hung over him like a cloud as he tried to start over in a new career, but now with four kids. At the midpoint of his life, Owen found himself reassessing his career, identity, and the overarching story of his life.

Many of us deeply enjoy our work. Yet we also feel lonely, anxious, tired, misunderstood, and undervalued at our jobs. In 2021 Gallup reported only 36 percent of US employees were engaged in their work and workplace; globally only 20 percent are engaged at work.[1] Much of the world is either going through the motions or lacking excitement for their current role.

The Covid-19 pandemic spurred millions to quit their jobs in 2021, popularly known as the Great Resignation. The mass layoffs of the 2020 pandemic lockdown, especially in restaurants and hotels, were clearly not forgotten by workers. When the economy began to recover a year later and employee power increased, millions walked out. In April 2021, four million Americans quit their jobs; in August, 65 percent of employees said they were looking for a new job.[2] Heather Long, a reporter at the *Washington Post*, believes the pandemic didn't just cause a labor shortage but "a great reassessment of work in America."[3]

As the reassessment of work becomes a stronger cultural current, we can't get away from the sense that if work is just exchanging dollars for hours, we're letting our lives slip away. Since the pandemic, a Pew Research Center study found the majority of workers who quit a job cited low pay, no opportunities for advancement, or disrespect as top reasons for leaving.[4] As jobs were plentiful, men and women across industries hit the door. And yet, the Great Resignation was often followed by "the Great Regret" for those same employees. Their next workplaces, many found, weren't much more human than the last ones.[5]

Finding meaning in work feels like searching for Bigfoot, ever elusive and probably just a myth. Owen and Brent are asking honest questions that many of us are too afraid to ask. Am I wasting my life? Is work meaningless? As I go about my daily life, *who am I becoming*?

A SPLINTERING CULTURE

Work is not done in a vacuum. The tensions around work in our culture are growing. Here are just a few.

The opportunity gap. Working-class communities are facing growing barriers to thriving lives. Since 1970, professional wages have increased dramatically, yet the wages of high school educated men have fallen 47 percent. You're more than twice as likely to die of suicide if you have a high school degree compared to a college degree. For kids of working-class parents, the rate of single-parent homes has jumped in the last half century from 20 to 70 percent. And shockingly, high-achieving poor kids are now *less* likely (29 percent) to get a college degree than low-achieving rich kids (30 percent). "This fact is particularly hard to square," writes Harvard sociologist Robert Putnam, "with the idea at the heart of the American Dream: equality of opportunity."[6]

Crisis of work. On one side of the economic spectrum, work has become almost a religion. Derek Thompson of the *Atlantic* calls this "workism," the belief that the center of one's identity and life's purpose must always be found in work.[7] On the other side is what researcher Nicholas Eberstadt calls America's invisible crises, the phenomenon of "men without work." As of the winter of 2020, "nearly 7 million civilian non-institutionalized men [not in prison] between the ages of 25 and 54 are neither working nor looking for work—over four times as many as are formally unemployed."[8] Arthur Brooks, a Harvard professor and former president of the American Enterprise Institute, points out that these men are not just lagging behind economically—they're experiencing a deficit of dignity.[9]

Social isolation. A Harvard study found more than one-third of all Americans—including 61 percent of young adults—report feeling "serious loneliness," which has worsened since the pandemic.[10]

Despite being more "connected" than ever through social media, researchers have pointed out that loneliness is more damaging to your health than smoking or obesity. Britain even appointed a minister for loneliness. The shift to remote or hybrid work after the pandemic accelerated this trend as well.

Mental health crisis. The United States surgeon general, Dr. Vivek H. Murthy, warns that young people are facing a "devastating" mental health crisis. Emergency room visits for suicide attempts rose 51 percent for adolescent girls in 2021. Yet trips to the ER related to depression, anxiety, and related issues were already up 28 percent from 2007 to 2018.[11] Anxiety rates are also rising for adults, especially Generation Z—individuals born from 1995 to 2010.[12]

Politicization of everything. We feel the politicization of nearly everything in our culture. From racial issues to social issues to workplace culture, much of it sits in a political container, which then turns up the heat on almost every conversation. Many churches, too, are being tugged to extremes by both pastors and congregants fearful of our cultural moment.

Decline of faith. In 1990, 87 percent of US adults identified as Christians. In 2009, that dropped to 77 percent; as of 2019, it was only 65 percent. Conversely, in 1990, 8 percent identified as "nones" or "religiously unaffiliated." In 2019, that number tripled to 26 percent. There are thirty million more "nones" in 2020 than just ten years ago.[13] Feeling like "the only Christian at work" is not just a feeling—it's a reality for millions.

Partisan fury, growing class divides, deepening social isolation, economic inequality, growing mental health issues, the decline of Christian belief in the West—as culture withers, many of us feel the stress of trying to live full, healthy lives.

Imagine a wine glass sitting on a countertop. Base, stem, bowl—a perfect container for a fine cabernet. It has *integrity*, which the dictionary defines as "the state of being whole and undivided." Now imagine bumping that glass onto the floor, where it shatters, its pieces scattering under the fridge, near the dining table, and throughout the kitchen. In this state, it has *disintegrated*, or "[broken] up into small parts, typically as the result of impact or decay." I'd argue that much of our contemporary culture has been disintegrating for some time.[14]

We rarely pause to reflect on the air we breathe, but a major reason our lives feel fragmented is that our culture is fractured. Covered by a thin veil of wealth and entertainment, we often feel stress without knowing why. As we move from the private space of home to the public space of work, we endure a thousand splinters of the day, only to go home feeling diminished, like "butter spread over too much bread," to borrow the words of J. R. R. Tolkien's Bilbo Baggins.

To live and work in this culture, we need a storyline that can bind together soul and system, mind and Monday, our work and our world.

WHICH STORY ABOUT WORK?

Culture tells us a story about work centered on our individual success. We will finally be happy with the title, the job, the salary. Of late, the story has shifted: we will finally be whole if we join the right cause and solve our world's social issues, while also obtaining flexibility, work-life balance, and a fun work environment (when I want to come to an office). Though there are things to praise about this shift, it still centers on *me*, trading career climbing for personal comfort.

Christians tell a different story about work. Christians say that since God himself works, and Adam and Eve were called into the Garden of Eden "to work it and care for it," work is intrinsically noble (Genesis 2:2, 5, 15). Many others, particularly in Reformed communities, also believe work is a charge to build and cultivate human civilization based on God's command to "Be fruitful and increase in number; fill the earth and subdue it" (Genesis 1:28). Work is good and a chance to impact culture.

Having shared this story probably hundreds of times, I heard honest critiques of this narrative about work as well. "Jeff, that's just high-minded idealism for people who've never had a real job in their lives." So I tell the other half of the biblical story about work: "Cursed is the ground because of you; through painful toil you will eat food from it all the days of your life" (Genesis 3:17). Genesis clearly paints a picture of the fall and how it's impacted our work, stretching from the "thorns and thistles" of daily labor to the monuments of human pride like the Tower of Babel (Genesis 11). Indeed, in the very field meant for farming, just a few verses after the fall, Cain kills his brother (Genesis 4:8), God reiterates the curse of work (Genesis 4:12), and the first technology, tools of bronze and iron, were likely forged for mining . . . and warfare (Genesis 4:22).

Work can feel creative, impactful, and important. Yet it can also feel like toil. "So I hated life, because the work that is done under the sun was grievous to me," says the author of Ecclesiastes. "All of it is meaningless, a chasing after the wind" (Genesis 2:17).

The truth is the Bible tells us *both* stories of work. Work was created good, but is now fallen. It is a way to cultivate the earth, yet can also corrupt the earth. Work is new business creation, teaching children to read, and works of art; it is also conflict with coworkers, being unjustly fired, and workplace injuries—both physical and spiritual.

The challenge for us today is to look squarely and honestly at the realities of work, and ask better, more honest questions. Not only, What work am I doing? but What is work doing to me?

Professional Versus Working-Class Perspectives

Work Identity Versus Communal Identity

In professional communities, workaholism and busyness is a sign of success. Missing a kid's football game or a family dinner is understandable, if it's for a deposition or board meeting. (Of course, far better to get to every soccer game, be fit, have a clean house, happy marriage, and have a successful, high-paying career.) For professionals, you are what you do. They derive their identity from their work.

But the working class dismiss work devotion as narcissism. One technician criticized professionals who are so "self-assured, so self-intense that they really don't care about anyone else. It's me, me, me."[15] Ambition is seen as trying to get ahead, a way to leave behind the community that cared for you in pursuit of personal success.

Instead, the working class prizes traditional family values and family loyalty. If you're from a professional family, moving to Silicon Valley is a fun opportunity. But if you sell toilets, it's safer to hang out with people who won't judge you for your dirty job. "Familiar faces provide a buffer against humiliation," writes Joan C. Williams, author of *White Working Class: Overcoming Class Cluelessness in America*.

"It's very easy for folks who have a lot of power to gravitate to Genesis 1 and 2 and the affirmation of the goodness of work," says Jim Mullins, a pastor at Redemption Tempe in Arizona. "In some ways that can become a proof text for what they already believe about work. On the same token, there are a lot of people in fields of work that are not esteemed by society that can tend to gravitate toward the Genesis 3 realities of work. They see work as toilsome, broken, and painful."[16]

Mullins believes "the temptation is to emphasize Genesis 1 and 2 with the powerful, and Genesis 3 with the vulnerable. But you see a deep transformation when you switch the emphasis." Working-class communities need to hear that work is a way to reflect God's image and cultivate creation; professionals need to hear that work is often unjust and in need of systemic redemption. They both need to know that neither work nor family is the foundational identity for the Christian, but Christ himself.

CRACKS IN MY ARMOR

We used to live in a two-bedroom townhouse behind a shopping mall. Between my wife, three kids and myself, it was a tight fit. One baby usually slept in a Pack-N-Play in the closet. But we felt grateful, like that rust red, split-level home with tile countertops was God's gift to us early in our married lives.

For years I worked at a Christian school during the day, but by night, I plotted out in a wire-bound notebook my own dream: an organization that helps people connect the gospel to the industries of our world. One evening in late 2012, I came home from work and my wife had rearranged a corner of our garage into an office, complete with a desk, lamp, printer, space heater, and pegboard sectioning off storage bins from the computer. "Honey, I believe you can do this," she said to me. "I'm for you." The tears welled up in my eyes. Her affirmation was just what I needed to hear.

And so I went for it. I spent a year recruiting a board, fundraising, building a plan, designing logos and eventually launching our first event, a gathering on faith and technology in one of America's most secular cities, Boulder, Colorado. In the first several years, even I was surprised by our success. We got our first grant, built a donor base, launched new events, developed a leadership program, and began to hire staff. From the outside, it looked all "up and to the right." Our budget was growing, our brand was starting to get recognition, and people I had never met somehow knew me.

But about five years in, I started to notice cracks in my armor. I would come home exhausted, with very little in the tank for my family, and often fall asleep an hour or two before my wife. When my kids needed discipline, I was sometimes very short-tempered, and then would quickly apologize, genuinely not knowing where my outburst came from. I noticed a feeling of near elation when we were "winning"—landing a large gift, hosting a successful event—and severe disappointment bordering on despair when I was rejected, slighted, or one of my plans flopped. I felt drawn to unhealthy patterns and a growing coldness within.

I noticed a growing divide between my exterior self and my interior self. My work persona (and LinkedIn profile) was all about success: growing influence, recognition, and public impact. But internally, I felt thin, lost, and concerned.

One day I pulled up to a stoplight in our family minivan. Waiting to cross the street was a thin White man, midtwenties, wearing baggy jeans, stained shoes, and a tattered tank top. He had buzzed hair, an unkept beard, bags under his eyes, and a cigarette hanging out his mouth. I said to my wife, who was sitting next to me, "Honey, I feel like that guy looks."

Rather than allowing faith to form my work, as my organization was built around, I felt like I had let my work *deform* me. Was this a calling from God, or had I simply baptized my own ambition? The world was cheering me on, but inside, I felt myself disengaging, disconnecting, and growing ever-wearier. I felt a growing need to shield those around me. And I had to ask myself a hard question: Was I a part of the solution for what's gone wrong in the world, or was I a part of the problem?

I've come to the conclusion that "faith and work" is not first about impact, success, or even a way to advance the gospel in the world— *it's about who we're becoming in the process of our working lives.*

Could there be a way to neither disengage from work, nor fall prey to the illusions of success, but instead live a truly healthy, whole life? A life that integrates and heals my heart and my mind, my work and my relationships, and the world around me?

SEARCHING FOR A PATH

This book is about asking honest questions about our lives and our work. It's also about seeking a path of transformation that binds together our interior lives, our exterior lives, and our communities.

Many Christians, I believe, are living their lives like the ancient Israelites in exile. Millions of Christians are like Israel, "who dwells among the nations; she finds no resting place" (Lamentations 1:3). We are anxious, lonely, and we lack a clear sense of purpose. The stats on this are all too pervasive. And yet, Jesus seems to be offering a different kind of life. He offers real interior freedom, and genuine rest for our souls as we "learn the unforced rhythms of grace" and "learn to live freely and lightly."

Could this kind of life be found in the actual realities of our families, communities, and even our work? Even amid the disappointments and setbacks we all experience in our families, our work, and dreams?

My conviction is that daily work is still central to both personal meaning and public contribution, and work is a way to fulfill Jesus' Great Commandment to love God and love others.

Finding a way to actually live into that conviction is a journey. It's a journey, I believe, that has the potential to transform us from the inside out.

2

From the Inside Out

No good tree bears bad fruit, nor does a bad tree bear good fruit.
Each tree is recognized by its own fruit. People do not pick figs
from thornbushes, or grapes from briers. A good man brings
good things out of the good stored up in his heart.

LUKE 6:43-45

"What does it mean for us to live love and actually encourage people?" asks Don Flow, a man in his late sixties with a wide smile and gentle eyes. "In biblical language, what will animate our culture? What will that really look like? The first thing for us has to be trust."

As a young man, Don decided not just to take over the family business but to first go to Regent College for his "faith to be grounded biblically and theologically." He then went to business school and afterward worked "every job" at Flow Automotive, including as a technician, doing oil changes, and working on intake manifolds. He wanted to understand his family business and the employees before he led.

Today Flow Companies has thirty-six car dealerships and fifteen hundred employees in North Carolina and Virginia. In an industry that makes money from "asymmetrical knowledge"—or knowing more than the customer—Don decided to deconstruct this business and build every practice around trust.

"Everything we do is about building trust with customers," Don says. Practically, this means giving customers only one estimate: "The ability to negotiate should not determine the price you pay." It also means being transparent with information. Rather than hiding information from customers, they've decided to make a profit through excellent service instead.

He says it also means serving customers—all of them—with integrity. Flow Automotive guarantees their repairs: "If we don't fix it right the first time, you never pay again." It also means putting a cap on finance so that lower-income customers don't pay more for their cars.

Don likens his attitude toward customers to how he'd treat a guest in his home: "If I was really going to treat a person like my neighbor, or like a guest in my home, that's what I would do."

For Don, trust means "keeping your promises always, regardless of the cost. It means you never advantage yourself by disadvantaging another."[1]

For Don, his interior world of faith and his exterior world of work are, like a solid bridge over a canyon, integrated and whole.

WHAT'S THE RECIPE?

Don Flow is an anomaly. In contrast to the fragmentation I've experienced in my own life, Don exudes unity in his mind, heart, work, relationships, and community influence. Thoughtful and gentle yet strong, he is a beautiful paradox. He's good at his work but cares more about love than "success." He's powerful yet not enamored with power. His influence has been large, but he seems largest when he gives you his focused, undivided attention.

Though Don and I have very different work lives and backgrounds, his example has given me pause. Work, rather than deforming him, seems to be *forming* him into somebody whole, contented, even joyful. When interviewing Don over the phone after an event where he spoke, I couldn't help but wonder: What's the recipe for such a vibrant, integrated life?

After ten years of interviewing hundreds of people about their work, I've tried to uncover this recipe for such a life of character. Who are the people living out this life of faith, and what are the principles that they share in common?

I've found that the vast majority of them have three convictions in common.

First, they embrace a broadened sense of the gospel. For many, religion fits in a small container of Sunday worship and devotionals, mostly serving to assure one's eternal destiny after death. For others, however, the *gospel* means the good news of Jesus' incarnation, death, resurrection and second coming, and his saving work for *everything, everyone, everywhere* (Colossians 1:15-20). The Bible paints a beautiful picture of the breadth of redemption summed up in the word *shalom*. God through Christ is healing our relationship with himself, with ourselves, with others, with culture and even with creation itself. This leads people to ask bigger questions about faith and their own work as ambassadors for God in a fallen world (1 Corinthians 5:19-20).

Second, they recognize culture is not neutral. We tend to think of culture as an unbiased space, with various religions having "biased" perspectives on, say, the news or their families. This is simply not true. Western culture has become deeply secular and functions much like a religion. The secular way of seeing centers the individual, dethrones authority, and attempts to segment faith apart from our work, our industries, and our civic life. But even our modern culture is filled with "gods."

Lesslie Newbigin, a British missionary to India for four decades, returned to his native England in the 1970s to a culture he barely recognized. He noted that rather than England being "neutral," it felt much more like Hindu India, with a thousand gods by other names, such as "my rights," the "free market," or "progress."[2]

"In the day-to-day trenches of adult life," said the late David Foster Wallace, "there is actually no such thing as atheism. There is no such thing as not worshipping. Everybody worships"—whether that be a Wiccan goddess, Vishnu, Jesus, power, success, money, or our children.[3] Culture is not neutral. Seeing the constant tug of philosophies, religions, and worldviews in a secular culture is key to seeing the "gods" in our companies, resisting those false gods, and finding a better way to live.

Third, they understand vocation as an entire life lived in response to the call of God. Though secular worldviews tend to draw sharp dividing lines between faith and work, private and public, values and facts, vocation is a unified way of seeing our faith and involvement in the world. Vocation is not just meaningful work or a type of schooling in the trades; it is the Christian's response to Jesus' Great Commandment to "love the Lord your God with all your heart and with all your soul and all your mind," and to "love your neighbor as yourself" (Matthew 22:37-39). Vocation is a moment-by-moment relationship *with* God, *for the benefit* of our neighbors, and *through* our daily work.[4]

The gospel is what God has done. Culture is where we find ourselves. And vocation is our response to God in the here and now.

FIVE GUIDING PRINCIPLES

Gospel, culture, and vocation build the concrete foundation of an integrated life for our emotions, minds, relationships, jobs, and involvement in society. I believe faith lived out in our working lives, then, is built around five principles: seek deep spiritual health, think theologically, embrace relationships, create good work, and serve others sacrificially.[5]

Seek deep spiritual health. Deep spiritual and emotional health is core to being fully human. In the midst of our widespread anxiety, depression, and mental health crisis, those who seek deep spiritual health decide to take the interior journey and open the shadows of their souls to the healing touch of God.

In 2016 Tracy Mathews started a new initiative on vocation, after rediscovering God's purposes for work in her career in business. She discovered over time her true interest was helping teams "cultivate spiritually attuned leadership." Though discerning God's will is mysterious for many, she believes it is arguably the most important skill for any person of faith working in business, government, or the social sector.

Tracy combined her experience with business teams and the classic spiritual disciplines to create Attune, a nonprofit that helps "teams grow in self-awareness, trust, and alignment as they process through the challenges and opportunities of work and leadership." Half business consultant and half spiritual director, she walks people through a process to listen, discern, act, and reflect on lived experiences, tracing the subtle movements of God in daily workplace decisions. For Tracy, the *way* we do our work is just as important as the outcome.

Because Christ called his disciples to "come follow me" and enter the kingdom of God, core to the life of faith is listening and submitting to the Holy Spirit, practicing the classic spiritual disciplines, and doing our work in a redemptive manner.

Think theologically. C. S. Lewis wrote in *The Weight of Glory*, "I believe in Christianity as I believe that the Sun has risen, not only because I see it but because by it, I see everything else."[6]

Thinking theologically means seeing everything—from agriculture to artificial intelligence to astronomy to abject failure—in light of the core teachings of Christian faith. This naturally moves faith into a space of open conversation and public witness because it's top-of-mind *for the actual work we do*. Rather than evangelism tactics that "change the topic" to Jesus around the office water cooler, the biblical story naturally forms the way we understand our careers, our coworkers, our companies, and our industries.

Jennifer Wiseman grew up in a rural area surrounded by nature. "I really loved wandering through forests, stomping around in streams, looking for wildlife, and looking up at the sky at night," she remembers. "The sky was pretty dark, so I was able to see lots of stars, and I was fascinated by them."[7] That fascination led to a lifelong passion. Today, Jennifer is a senior astrophysicist at the NASA Goddard Space Flight Center and the senior project scientist for the Hubble Space Telescope.

Even though Jennifer works at the intersection of two very secular fields—science and government—she sees her role as an advocate for scientific discovery in light of her faith as a Christian. "We should use our dominion to be stewards," she says, referencing the cultural mandate in Genesis, "stewards of what we can touch on our own planet Earth and then stewards of this knowledge that God is enabling us to have through science. For Christians, that should give us a deeper, richer sense of amazement of God's creation. And we should use this knowledge to help others be awestruck and liven their spirits."

Jennifer sees her work as an astronomer as a project to point people to the Creator. She does this through encouraging the church toward a sense of wonder as well as hosting dialogues on science, ethics, and religion for the American Association for the Advancement of Science and for BioLogos, a Christian advocacy group that supports conversations and research around creation, evolution, science, and faith.

Jennifer's faith is not segmented off from her work, but instead it is a source of understanding and inspiration for her work. In this approach to faith and work, theology is not merely esoteric or ethereal. It's a central source of knowledge, insight, and practice for daily work, whether in astrophysics or lesson planning, carpentry or customer service.

As stewards of the mysteries of Christ, Christians seek to understand how Scripture, the historic church, and the gospel of grace influence our work and cultural engagement.

Embrace relationships. In contrast to the social isolation and loneliness in our culture, God himself is loving relationship—Father, Son, and Holy Spirit. In the incarnation, Jesus drew physically near (John 1:14), giving us a vision of how relationships are central to our lives. In-person, around-the-table, laughing-and-crying relationships is what humans long for. We were designed for relationship.

And yet, relational work is hard work. It means growing in self-awareness, navigating the personality traits of others, and continually giving and forgiving. In particular, relationships with coworkers, clients, and bosses are continually some of the greatest stressors of our working life.

It's through daily participation in the divine relationship of the Trinity that we find the strength to extend that life to others (1 Peter 1:4). Those who choose to embrace relationships see people as an end in themselves, not a means. They embrace healthy friendships, cultivate institutional strength with coworkers by committing to their organization's core mission, and care about others in practical ways out of a commitment to neighbor love.

Dave Meyer is a perfect example of embracing relationships. "All I did was smile at him from the bus driver's seat," says Dave, who served as a school bus driver for Cherry Creek School District in Colorado for eight years. Dave tells me the story at a church BBQ of a student walking on the sidewalk, whom he found out was missing his father, who still lived in China. Giving him a simple smile as he got on the bus one day turned into getting to know his family, visiting car shows together, and forming a friendship.

For Dave, core to living out his faith in his work is relationships. Previously he worked as an engineer, but he felt God's call to work with children. "It became apparent to me that God's love is big enough to encompass all the people in the district and all the kids we touch each day," he said, referring to the ten cities in his school district and the fifty-one thousand students it serves, including twenty-four hundred special needs students. "One day, I spoke to other bus drivers about our jobs. So many people just see this job as a paycheck."

"But I said to them, 'When a kid walks onto your bus, each and every one of them is important. They're not just a paycheck—each of them has a unique story and life. We have a responsibility to greet them with a smile and take care of them.'"[8]

The doctrines of the Trinity and the incarnation lead us to deeply value face-to-face conversations, long-term friendships, and redemptive relationships between individuals, organizations, and churches.

Professional Versus Working-Class Perspectives

Creativity Versus Dependability

Professionals value entrepreneurial initiative, boundary breaking, and creativity. They signal initiative by "breaking the rules." But the working-class values dependability and stability, which are useful dispositions if you're an order-taker rather than an order-maker. For example, at Weifield Group Electrical Contracting, management says there are three characteristics of successful electrical apprentices: show up on time, have a good attitude, and be willing to learn. Creativity just might get you electrocuted.

> Professionals tend to ask about their work, How can I stay inspired? The working class asks, How can I keep my job and eventually get a raise?
>
> Here, working-class workers and professionals can learn from each other. God calls people to the creative use of their gifts (1 Peter 4:10; Genesis 2:15) as well as to a life of faithfulness, particularly in painful circumstances (most of the Bible). Working-class communities can teach professionals about what it means to show up, do what you'd rather not do, and stay faithful to your commitments. Professionals can teach working-class workers about what it takes to imagine a new business, challenge societal norms, or explore new possibilities.[9] Both can learn from Christ, who is both creative and faithful (John 1:3; Hebrews 3:2).

Create good work. God worked for six days and rested for one. We were created in his image, and minimally that means that we too are made to be creators and workers (Genesis 1–2).

Christian faith invites us to see our lives and work in light of God's good creation, the resurrection of Christ, and the promised new heaven and new earth. The physical world that we change, shape, and form through our work has inherent value because God made it and will one day redeem it (1 Corinthians 15:58). Those who adopt this vision for work spread healthy motives for their work, grow in professional competence, and experience deep coherence between their work and their faith.

Hilary Oswald is a kind of creator. With a vibrant wit, an eye for detail, and a true delight in other people's stories, Hilary's work as a journalist covers topics ranging from design and architecture to health. While Hilary writes stories for faith-based organizations, most of her writing would be considered "secular." Yet she doesn't see it that way.

"As a Christian, I think homes are gifts and tools," Hilary says about her writing for *5280 Home*, a lifestyle magazine serving Denver. Her articles describe custom interiors, custom kitchens, and artist-inspired homes. "I try to explicitly and implicitly convey the life behind a home and the value of hospitality."

Her writing is *itself a good thing*, apart from any explicitly religious content, because she believes this world is ultimately God's world. Just as the mountains on Denver's horizon don't explicitly say "I am God the Creator," Hilary's writing gently points people to a deeper beauty and a love for God's world. "God is where all the beautiful things come from. . . . When we turn chaos into order, when we invest in beauty, we reflect a little bit of who God is."[10]

Embracing God's creation and the hope of the resurrection, an integrated faith values Spirit-filled labor, a commitment to craftsmanship, and projects that serve as a sign and foretaste of God's coming kingdom.

Serve others sacrificially. In a cultural context of growing economic disparities,[11] hyper-partisanship, and a secularizing environment, those who serve others sacrificially bring their faith to their work through acts of compassion and justice. They give generously of their resources, work to heal the divisions in society, and address big issues ranging from poverty and addiction to opportunity for low-income communities. Rather than triumphantly conquering culture, Christians see sacrificial love as the central way we reflect faith to an unbelieving world.

Not long ago, I spent a day with Karla Nugent, the cofounder of Weifield Group Contracting, a commercial electrical company in Denver. She led me into the prefabrication shop. Coils, wires, and electrical boxes were being assembled for installation. We met Scott Ammon, a journeyman electrician at Weifield Group, who shared his story: "I'd actually been suffering from PTSD while I was there," after serving in the US Army in Desert Storm and then for eleven years in the US Postal Service. As a result, he'd struggled with drug addiction and spent two years at the Stout Street Foundation, an alcohol and drug rehabilitation facility.

During rehab, Scott heard about an opening for an electrical apprentice at Weifield. The four-year program trains employees in a prefabrication process (preparing electrical materials for on-site installation) while paying for their education to become state-certified journeymen electricians. "I was really nervous when [Karla] interviewed me because I was in treatment at the time," Scott recalled, figuring he'd be passed over because of his struggle with substance abuse. "But she looked me straight in the eyes and just nodded her head." When he got the offer despite his rocky past, he felt rewarded. "I said to myself, 'From now on, they've got my full dedication.'"

Karla cofounded Weifield in 2002 alongside three business partners. Since then, the company has grown to over 250 employees and emerged at the forefront of electrical construction. In 2014, Karla won the *Denver Business Journal*'s Corporate Citizen of the Year Award as well as the award for Outstanding Woman in Business for architects, engineers, and construction. But light began to flood into Weifield when, several years ago, she decided to bring the community's needs *into* the company through creating an apprenticeship program that gives people like Scott a second chance.[12] Her work, she believes, is a way to care for both her co-workers and her community.

To be a Christian is to embrace a call to costly discipleship, high levels of commitment, acts of sacrificial service, and courageous public witness. Christians heed the call to biblical justice and serve the needs of the poor and marginalized in our work and communities. And as the body of Christ for the life of the world, Christians press into contemporary problems, adopt a broad perspective in addressing complex and systemic issues, and pursue shalom in all areas of society.

EVERY CORNER

Seek deep spiritual health, think theologically, embrace relationships, create good work, and serve others sacrificially—this is a vision of holistic discipleship that influences our work and our world.

SEEK DEEP SPIRITUAL HEALTH   **EMBRACE RELATIONSHIPS**   **CREATE GOOD WORK**

THINK THEOLOGICALLY   **SERVE OTHERS SACRIFICIALLY**

Dallas Willard once wrote, "The greatest issue facing the world today, with all its heartbreaking needs, is whether those who, by profession or culture, are identified as 'Christians' will become disciples—students, apprentices, practitioners—of Jesus Christ, steadily learning from him how to live the life of the Kingdom of the Heavens into every corner of human existence."[13] I've always been inspired by such statements. Yet "every corner of human existence" has always felt intimidating to me. I'm the kind of person who can't even do this every moment of a single day—or hour.

And yet, I do believe it's possible. Knowing what Jesus knows about each of us, would he have intended otherwise?

I've come to believe that a vibrant, whole life—toward something like the simple joyfulness of Don Flow—can actually be lived out in the reality of our lives, even in the most everyday of activities, like selling used cars. "Faith is something we actually exercise, it's not an abstraction," Don says. "Love is something we actually live. And hope is actually something we bring."

The idea of this book is to give us a place to start this journey of living in relationship with God in all areas of life. First, we need to focus not on the world's problems but on our own hearts and minds, seeking deep spiritual and emotional health and theological truth. Second, we allow inner transformation to affect our core relationships and our work. And finally, our work and relationships influence our cities and the big issues in our culture. God is healing the world first through our interior life, second through our exterior life, and third through our civic life.

The beginning of the journey starts in the depths of the human heart. Jesus said, "No good tree bears bad fruit, nor does a bad tree bear good fruit. Each tree is recognized by its own fruit. People do not pick figs from thornbushes, or grapes from briers. A good man brings good things out of the good stored up in his heart" (Luke 6:43-45). Can we—deeply, truly—become good in the recesses of our souls?

The journey of living and working from the inside out starts with each of us being willing to take step one, which for me is by far the hardest: seek deep spiritual health.

PART 2

Reintegration

3

Seek Deep
Spiritual Health

Stand at the crossroads and look; ask for the ancient paths, ask where the good way is, and walk in it, and you will find rest for your souls.

JEREMIAH 6:16

Not long ago, my weekend turned into a complete disaster.

I received word on a Friday afternoon in January that I didn't hit an important work goal the previous year. I woke up Saturday morning loaded with anxiety. I told my wife, "I'm sorry, but I'm so anxious right now I need to work for a couple of hours. Then I'll be better."

So I drove to a local Starbucks and dove in. After two hours of looking at data, the anxiety was even worse. I felt terrible. I was concerned what my mistake might cost me and others. My breath was getting short. A tingling sensation ran up my neck.

Throughout the day, as the stress grew, my behavior began to deteriorate. I was short-tempered with my kids and distant from my wife. I felt the draw of temptation clearly. That evening, my wife made us some pizza and said, "Let's watch a movie." We talked about a few movie choices for the kids to take their pick.

In about sixty seconds my kids started arguing about which movie, and I barked, "Then no movie!" My six-year-old screamed at me, "No dad!" At that moment, I looked at her and I thought fire was going to come out of my nose and ears.

I took my pizza, went into my bedroom, and slammed the door. I had to sequester myself away from my family out of concern I was going to really hurt somebody I love. As I sat alone in my room, eating pizza on an unmade bed, I said, "God, what is wrong with me?"

NOTICING WHAT'S THERE

One morning not long after the pizza-explosion episode, I was looking in the mirror and thinking about the hundreds of hours I had spent in Bible studies, at church services, and at seminary. And yet I could still erupt in rage. I could still burn with envy and spout off prideful remarks. I could still get pulled into addictive behavior. I know so much about God and the Bible, but how much did I really know about myself? I could answer the question, who is God? But I couldn't answer the question, who am I? I was reminded of what John Calvin, the French Reformer, wrote in his *Institutes of the Christian Religion*: "Our wisdom, insofar as it ought to be deemed true and solid Wisdom, consists entirely of two parts: the knowledge of God and of ourselves."

My journey toward spiritual and emotional health began in a paradoxical place—by admitting there's pain within that I can't heal by myself. And all I can do is start to *notice* what's happening, verbalize it, and take the first step in coming to see myself as I really am.

Psychiatrist and author Curt Thompson says, "Guilt is something I feel because I have done something bad. Shame is something I feel because I *am* bad."[1] Shame causes us to hide, as we saw in the Garden of Eden after Adam and Eve ate the fruit (Genesis 3:7). Being "naked" and without defense is terrifying; it takes deep courage to *see* both the good and bad inside of us and *not try to fix it*, which is often simply another mechanism for self-defense and self-justification.

"One night when my children were eight, six, and five, I was putting them to bed and they started to complain they hadn't done anything fun that day," recalled David Park, a Korean American businessman and real estate investor. "And I absolutely laid into them. For as loud as I could and as long as I could, I yelled at them, backing them into a corner of the room, where they huddled together weeping in fear. I remember thinking I wanted to intentionally scar them so they would remember how entitled they are."

David grew up in a Korean family that went through generations of pain, from Japanese colonialism to the Korean War. The pressure to perform felt like life or death. It worked: David had two degrees from elite universities and a high-octane career. He also had emotions he didn't understand and couldn't control. He went on to share, "When I finished yelling, my wife told me very clearly, 'You need to get some help.' And I knew she was right. That day had been a long time coming, and I knew it wouldn't get better if I didn't deal with what was really causing the anger."[2]

David's story echoes my own, as both show that inner healing starts with admitting there's a problem, and rather than judging and "fixing," simply *noticing* what is happening internally and externally. We avoid this process of acceptance and reflection because we fear that we'll not only see that we've done wrong but also feel that we are beyond redemption.

To be vulnerable before God and others, as David was when sharing his story, is the beginning of change. Though there are many important secular tools and therapies available to begin this healing process, only Christian faith offers the foundational truth of unconditional acceptance and grace. God himself embraces us right now as we are, even in the midst of our illness, brokenness, and pain. It is safe to bring our darkest thoughts to the surface because,

> The LORD your God is with you,
>   the Mighty Warrior who saves.
> He will take great delight in you;
>   in his love he will no longer rebuke you,
>   but will rejoice over you with singing. (Zephaniah 3:17)

Grace is the foundation for paying attention and honestly looking at your sin and distortion, and yet seeing yourself as one whom God loves.

FROM VULNERABILITY TO SELF-AWARENESS

The safety of God's unconditional love opens the door to the hard, wild journey of self-awareness. For those willing to take the journey, there are multiple tools for growing in self-awareness.

For example, as a part of a biannual review process, the staff at Denver Institute for Faith & Work regularly do 360-degree reviews. On the face of it, they're straightforward enough. You ask your direct report, your coworkers, and those who report to you two sets of questions. First, "What does it look like when I'm at my best? What gifts am I demonstrating? What strengths are being underutilized? What impact do I have on people?" And second, "What are three gaps or weaknesses that may be limiting my effectiveness?" The second part intentionally uses softer language because of how hard it is to give and receive honest feedback.

Here are three honest comments from my friends, family, and coworkers that were hard for me to receive:

- "Listen . . . work on *active* listening. Work to ensure that your (usually wise and interesting!) stream of thought doesn't plow over inputs and interjections of others."

- "I would encourage you to do some hard but needed work to understand the impact you have on others relationally. My own experience is that you come across as transactional and noncollaborative."

- "Your high-achieving and perfectionistic tendencies make you a natural leader. I encourage you to work toward allowing those around you to be less than perfect but still wholly accepted and affirmed by you."

When I first read these, I intellectually knew these people loved me and wanted to see me grow. But inside I also simmered. *Don't they know how much I do around here? Aren't they grateful for everything I do?* For me it is a constant challenge to truly listen to others, notice what I'm feeling, and hang on to my unchanging identity in Christ without cascading into a pit of self-condemnation.

Often in the midst of relational stress or tension, I remember Father Thomas Keating's "Welcoming Prayer": "I let go of my desire for power and control. I let go of my desire for affection, esteem, approval and pleasure. I let go of my desire for survival and security. I let go of my desire to change any situation, condition, person or myself. I open myself to the love and presence of God and God's action within me." It's prayers like this that allow me to grow in self-awareness by not responding with anxiety, worry, or even resentment to negative feedback. I can listen because ultimately I know that I have everything I need in God (Psalm 23:1).

Those who grow in self-awareness take stock of what they are and what they're not. They look squarely at their talents and their limitations. They realize they won't change the world. But they also realize that they *can* change the world right around them—coworkers, community, church, and family. And perhaps even more importantly, they become okay with knowing and working with people who are richer, smarter, better looking, and more talented. Seeking approval for performance is calmed by the unwavering approval of God.[3]

It takes courage to take the interior journey. But shifting the focus from exterior markers of success to personal questions about character is core to finding deep, lasting emotional and spiritual health.

DESIRE, HABITS, AND WORKPLACE CULTURE

Work is forming us. I've seen it happen in my life and in hundreds of those I've had the privilege of knowing.

Take, for example, Alan, Angela, and Terry. For years Alan Chan worked as a corporate lawyer in a public company that was always pressing for quarterly results. Returns for shareholders caused a constant treadmill of stress-fueled production, trickling down from the C-suite to the cleaning crew. He felt the drive for production shaping his habits, his mood, and his relationships. Angela Evans recently stepped down from her job as an editor at the *Boulder Weekly*. "I was just burned out," she said, needing space to breathe apart from a deadline. Angela saw, too, that work was good but also deformative. Terry Looper's experience was similar. "I realized I was addicted to the deal," said Terry, the founder of a large energy company. The elation of success functioned like a culturally approved addiction, yet it wasn't helping him or his employees flourish.[4] From worrying about money to being constantly connected through our phones, work shapes our minds, bodies, and hearts.

Pursuing Christian spiritual formation apart from considering how our work and daily life are already forming us is like asking cars to swim or fish to fly. Our daily environment is deeply formative. It quietly sets the horizon for who we become. For example, if everybody smokes while on break to deal with stress, in time you might smoke too. If Elon Musk is seen as a superhero among your peers, you might find yourself consuming *Entrepreneur* magazine on the weekends. And if you work in a hospital, it'll likely influence every-thing from your view of health insurance to your eating habits.

The trick is to notice not just habits but loves. Industries, like people, are all directed toward things we ultimately love. Fyodor Dostoevsky, the Russian novelist, believed this so much that he thought people were ultimately worshipers who seek some all-encompassing love. "So long as man remains free, he strives for nothing so incessantly and so painfully as to find someone to worship," he wrote in *The Brothers Karamazov*. Humans crave not just worship, Dostoyevsky believed, but a "community of worship" that "all would believe in."[5]

As a result, we create institutions, organizations, and businesses that look almost . . . religious. One large public company in Denver, as a part of training new hires, asks them to cross a literal bridge as a final initi-ation rite in embracing their company's mission and values. The tech industry loves the big "exit" (sale of a company or initial public offering); the military loves strength, discipline, and honor; the academy loves big brains and publications.[6] Our workplaces shape our desires, our desires shape our habits, and our habits shape our characters.

When we notice what our industry or company loves, we can pause to evaluate: Which of these things do I really love too?

Desire is not all bad. Actually, God created us to desire. C. S. Lewis wrote, "It would seem that Our Lord finds our desires not too strong, but too weak. We are half-hearted creatures, fooling around with drink and sex and ambition when infinite joy is offered us."[7] Key to our spiritual growth is not to deny what we desire but to reorder our desires. Thinkers ranging from Saint Augustine to contemporary voices like philosopher James K. A. Smith and *New York Times* col-umnist David Brooks believe we change when we *elevate* our loves.[8] When we, for instance, start to love a job well done more than a big title, or the promotion of a colleague more than a big paycheck, then we become more human. When the experience of God and the good of our neighbor is our highest love, then we become truly alive (Matthew 22:36-40).

One way we can gauge how we're doing is by paying attention to how hard it is to let go, especially of things we really care about. How do you feel when you get a promotion? And how about when you're passed over? How do you feel when you have the money to buy a delicious dinner, and how about when you don't? How do you feel when your plans succeed? How about when they fail? To gently let go of temporary things and situations allows us to grasp onto Christ, the one obsession we can dive wholeheartedly into without danger.

Saint Ignatius of Loyola taught the difference between being enslaved by things and receiving them as gifts intended to draw our hearts ultimately to God. Attachment, thought Ignatius, is a clinging and grasping onto the created world, which leads to slavery, bondage, and death. In contrast, "active indifference" is not carelessness but a holding of God's good gifts in freedom, able to receive or let go. When we do this, "everything has the potential of calling forth in us a deeper response to our life in God." The difference between active indifference and disengaged apathy is simply joy. Active indifference breeds interior freedom and love; disengaged apathy multiplies sloth and despair. "Our only desire and our one choice should be this: I want and I choose what better leads to the deepening of God's life in me."

Jack Kim is a commercial real estate investor based in Denver, Colorado, and an example of active indifference worth emulating. He often spends months putting together a "deal," which for Jack means analyzing and finding a commercial or apartment building to buy, co-investing with a group of investors, and working with lawyers, financial analysts, real estate brokers and others to "go after a building." Sometimes, after months of work and tens of thousands of dollars invested, the whole thing falls apart. "Often all I can do is hold my hands open before God," says Jack, recounting how he deals with disappointment. "What's important is that I don't grasp onto my work and clutch my hands, but leave them open for God to either give it to me or take it away." True freedom for Jack doesn't come from accumulating or acquiring but instead acting as a steward rather than an owner. Though difficult when a vision doesn't materialize, Jack practices active indifference in his work as a way to pursue interior freedom.[9]

Work is forming us, and so are our industries. But the key to allowing work to shape us into Christ's image is to "appreciate and use these gifts of God insofar as they help us toward our goal of loving service and union with God. But insofar as any created things hinder our progress toward our goal, we ought to let them go."[10] When God's gifts displace God as the center of our lives, we will find freedom releasing them and resetting our desire once more on God himself. "It is for freedom that Christ set us free" (Galatians 5:1).

LEARNING THE RHYTHMS OF GRACE

December 14, 2021, was a beautiful day. With 7:35 left in the first quarter, Stephen Curry, the legendary point guard for the Golden State Warriors, broke the NBA all-time three-point record.

As a basketball fan, I watched the YouTube video over and over in the coming days. It was in Madison Square Garden against the New York Knicks. He popped out of the lane, received the pass, and with his signature quick release, *swoosh*. The crowd rose to their feet in awe. Curry hit his 2,974th three-point shot, and he did it in just 789 games, 511 fewer than the previous record holder, Ray Allen.

Now, we'd like to say that Curry is just a natural shooter. And certainly, Curry has a unique feel for the game. But Curry also combined understanding the science of the three-point shot with dedication to training and repetition. He became great not through luck or even desire but committed practice.

Similarly, we grow into deep spiritual health not just through ideas or good intentions but through practice.

When I was a new Christian, one of the first things I learned from my involvement in campus ministry was that Christians often have a daily quiet time. This usually involved structured Bible reading, perhaps a devotional book, and—if I was particularly motivated or had the time—a list of prayer requests.

Daily devotions worked for me for years, but over time, I grew tired of them. I had read the stories, done the prayers, experimented with dozens of devotional books. For a long time, I fell away from morning devotionals. And for years I felt a deep sense of shame. Was I failing? What was wrong with my spiritual life? Had God abandoned me—or had I abandoned him?

In this time of asking questions, my former colleague Brian Gray quietly, persistently reintroduced to me the rich Christian tradition that I had overlooked. For so many years I had seen spiritual disciplines as restrictive, even potentially un-Protestant. Wasn't I simply saved by grace?

I'm slowly beginning to realize that spiritual disciplines are like a trellis, as Peter Scazzero says in his wonderful book *Emotionally Healthy Spirituality*. A trellis is a structure for vines to grow on. They don't *cause* the plant's growth; they *support* the growth. In the same way, spiritual disciplines are the trellis on which the Holy Spirit grows his fruit in our lives. Prayer, sabbath, confession, simplicity, solitude, celebration— these are the structures on which the Spirit climbs into our hearts and penetrates our emotions in the process of sanctification.[11]

Paul writes, "Physical training is of some value, but godliness has value for all things" (1 Timothy 4:8). Paul is probably not thinking of spiritual practices in isolation from the real, difficult work of daily living. We were always meant to live the spiritual life in and through our real, daily life.

For example, breath prayers—simple, one-sentence prayers that can be repeated through the day—can be said quietly at an office or in a factory. "Speak, for your servant is listening" (1 Samuel 3:10). Or after you lose your temper with a coworker: "Have mercy on me, Lord Jesus Christ, Son of David, for I am a sinner." The practices of listening for God's voice can be done through *lectio divina*, or meditative reflection on Scripture, while on the way to work.

One month-by-month guide to the spiritual disciplines suggests taking a month to be intentional with nonbelievers at your place of work through simply spending time together and recognizing the contributions of your coworkers.[12]

Whether it's sabbath rest or confession, the spiritual life must be practiced. Christians are apprentices to Jesus, asking him what it looks like to live in the kingdom of heaven and then taking action. It's not the outcome of our work that God is most interested in. It's who we become in the process. And this is less a life working *for* God and more one working *alongside* Christ, our ever-present friend.[13]

DELIGHT

The next morning after my alone-in-the-room-pizza meltdown, I stumbled out of bed, got a coffee, and sat on my brown leather chair. I felt a sense of shame for how I had behaved the day before, remembering the anger, isolation, and utter lack of self-control I displayed before my wife and four daughters.

About ten minutes later, one of my daughters, Lily, came up the stairs. Bedhead and groggy, she just smiled and sat next to me. Then she had an idea. She went into her room and came back with her slime kit. It was Sunday morning before church and she started to mix slime.

Now, I'm not a huge fan of slime, especially the kind with dyes (that also dye carpet, furniture, and clothes). But for a moment, I just watched. She was working away at our kitchen countertop, with the sun's rays gently shining on her through the window. As I sat there, sipping my coffee and looking at my daughter, all of a sudden I felt this powerful sense of *delight* in her. It wasn't that her work of creating slime was particularly impressive. But she was mine, and I was just delighted that she existed and that she was in my presence.

And then I thought, what if God feels this same sense of delight in me right now? I had a hard time believing this, based on my behavior the day before. But the thought persisted.

Because I'm a skeptic at heart, I thought, *Okay, it's easy to feel delight in my daughter when she's being good, but what about when she's in the back of our van punching a sister in the back, or complaining, or being selfish? What would I say then? Well, I'd certainly discipline her in the moment, for her good and her sister's. But would I love her any less?* The answer to that question was obvious.

As I took another sip of coffee, I imagined what God would say to my daughter in that moment when she was at her worst. Again, I had a powerful impression that God would say something like, "Oh my dearest. That's not who you really are. I know who you are. Let my love transform you. And no matter what comes, I'll be patient with you. I delight in you."

I felt myself come to a crossroads. Something shifted in my heart. I looked out at the morning sun, through our unwashed window pane. I smiled.

It was Sunday morning.

4

Think Theologically

For with you is a fountain of life;
in your light we see light.

PSALM 36:9

"You know, most of the time you'd look at picking up trash as being negative. It's like, 'Do I really have to do this?'" says Dave Lopes, a facilities coordinator at Colorado Community Church in Aurora, Colorado. As we go outside, he tells me about walking the parking lot, which the church shares with a strip mall, and picking up litter each morning. His daily responsibilities include event setup, building safety, repair, and cleaning.

Yet his vision for his work isn't only about maintenance. In contrast to how many might view his job, Dave sees a different reality. "As I spend time with God meditating, worshiping, and thanking him, he shows me the sins of the world and how Jesus' sacrifice on the cross is sufficient for our sins." Dave re-envisions the parts of his job he doesn't like. "Like the mess I see each morning, our sins are everywhere. And so, as I pick up this trash, I just see God cleansing me—and the world."[1]

For Dave, Christian doctrine is not just relegated to the concerns of pastors, priests, and professors. He sees doctrines not only as nice ideas but as new ways to frame his life—all of his life—including his work. Scripture, theology, and church history are not simply academic pursuits. They're a fountain of life and the light through which he sees and transfigures all the "normal" activities, even picking up trash on a Monday morning.

THE AIR WE BREATHE

"We take captive every thought to make it obedient to Christ," writes Paul to the church in Corinth (2 Corinthians 10:5). Thoughts are a part of our interior world, a realm that Christ is making new. Christians two thousand years ago, as well as Christians today, were bombarded with lies, half-truths, worldviews, philosophies, idols, and religions that claim for themselves ultimate authority.

In our twenty-first-century Western culture, we often drastically underestimate how secular our society really is. Seattle sure feels different from South Georgia, but increasingly secularism is the air we breathe.

What exactly do we mean by the word *secular*? Long ago, before the modern age, secular used to simply mean "everyday" tasks like farming, domestic work, or selling goods at a market, in contrast to "priestly" tasks like preaching or giving the sacraments.

Today we can best understand the word *secular* in two ways. The first is what philosopher Charles Taylor calls "exclusive humanism."[2] It's not just that people are abandoning belief in God (though many are) or that religion is marginalized outside of places of worship or the home (though it is). *Secular* here simply means that our culture systematically excludes any explanation of the world that isn't built around humans or human action. God simply isn't "real" like a desk, a corporation, or a law is real. It's often seen as inappropriate to reference God as a subject that can be known, like physics or the rules of pickleball. A secular culture explains our world exclusively in human terms.

The vast majority of our workplaces are just this: secular.

Abraham Nussbaum, a psychiatrist at Denver Health, Denver's largest public hospital, gave me a tour of the hospital grounds. A bench near the entrance of the hospital has an inscription of a familiar—yet incomplete—phrase: "Do justice, love mercy and walk humbly." The quote is from Micah 6:8 but is missing the phrase "with your God." Many hospitals in the United States, Abraham explained, were founded by Christians, hence the name "Saint" in many hospital names. Yet in the twentieth century, a confluence of factors, including the corporatization of health care, led to the secularization of the industry. God might be in the hearts of patients or in the prayers of chaplains, but references to the divine will rarely be found in diagnoses, prescriptions, or treatment plans. The "real" work of healing must be done with humans and by humans, without assuming any divine interference.

The second way to see secularism is more like polytheism, or the belief in many gods. This can be better understood through a story told by Lesslie Newbigin, a twentieth-century British theologian who served as a missionary in India. He writes,

> When I was a young missionary, I used to spend one evening each week in the monastery of the Ramakrishna Mission in the town where I lived, sitting on the floor with the monks and studying with them the Upanishads and the Gospels. . . .
>
> In the great hall of the monastery, as in all the premises of the Ramakrishna Mission, there is a gallery of portraits of the great religious teachers of humankind. Among them, of course, is a portrait of Jesus.
>
> Each year on Christmas Day worship was offered before this picture. Jesus was honored, worshipped, as one of the many manifestations of deity in the course of human history. To me,

as a foreign missionary, it was obvious that this was not a step toward the conversion of India. It was the co-option of Jesus into the Hindu worldview.

Jesus had become just one figure in the endless cycle of karma and samsara, the wheel of being we are all caught up in. He had been domesticated into the Hindu worldview.[3]

In the same way, a secular society doesn't lack gods; it has millions. Everybody has a set of ultimate beliefs they live by. Sometimes they're defined religions, like Islam or Judaism. More often, however, they are faith in either government or the free market, an absolute devotion to one's kids or one's profession, or a "religious" commitment to a Netflix series or a political ideology.

Like the Hindu worldview with its many gods, secular societies too have many gods and goddesses, and Jesus can be co-opted into a pantheon chosen by the individual. In America today, as Christianity wanes, we don't live in a "secular atheist" culture, where no god is worshiped, but instead in a "secular pluralist" culture, where every god is worshiped.

Recently I was driving down South Broadway on my way home from work. As I passed the Baker neighborhood, I was entertained by the mosaic of life lining the street: antique shops, graffiti on the walls, pot shops, and gas stations. As I came to a stoplight, I couldn't help but notice the interesting mix of bumper stickers on a black Land Rover in front of me.

There were three stickers heralding ski slopes in Moab and Vail, a Colorado State University sticker, and a sticker that said, "You can go fast, I can go anywhere." Above them all was a white sticker outlining the figure of a woman in high heels that says, "She thinks my Land Rover is sexy." And finally in the lower right corner, just above the bumper, a Jesus fish.

I couldn't help but see the parallels between Newbigin's story and my cultural context in outdoor-loving Colorado. America too has a pantheon that welcomes many gods—as long as you don't claim, "I am the LORD, and there is no other" (Isaiah 45:5).

We live in a culture immersed in a secular worldview that excludes God from any answer (or question), while simultaneously worshiping anything and everything. The task for Christians is to think theologically, or to see all of reality in light of the biblical story.

INSIDE THE RIGHT STORY

It takes real intentionality to question the storyline that's driving your work or industry and to try to see your daily activities in light of reality, the world revealed by Scripture.

Robin John, the cofounder of Eventide Asset Management, is doing the hard work of thinking theologically. When newspaper reporters would interview Robin, a subtle snicker rumbled below the surface. One called him "The Believer"; another pointed out the odd language on his website: business as an "engine of blessing" and "investing that makes the world rejoice." Theology as the foundation for picking stocks? Is this guy for real?

Robin was an early leader in the growing faith-based investing movement, a community that draws wisdom from Scripture for investing. The early days of the movement focused on screening out "vice stocks"—pornography, tobacco, weapons, or abortion—and then looking for financial gain. "It's a good start," says Robin, "but it doesn't go far enough because businesses can harm not just through bad products but through bad practices."

Robin believes the biblical language for these businesses is plunder, citing God's concern for the vulnerable,

"Because the poor are plundered and the needy groan,
  I will now arise," says the LORD.
"I will protect them from those who malign them."
    (Psalm 12:5)

But at Eventide, they took it a step further and asked more basic questions. What's God's purpose for our work? How about for business? And how would that influence what businesses we invest in?

Instead of merely avoiding companies that plunder or extract value from a community, Robin says, "we look for companies with an extraordinary ability to innovate and create value for all stakeholders." Eventide cofounders Jason Myhre, Finny Kuruvilla, and Robin believe business is a way to fulfill Jesus' Great Commandment to "love your neighbor as yourself," and the best businesses to invest in are not necessarily those with the best short-term gains but those that provide unique benefit to the six "neighbors" of a business: customers, employees, suppliers, host communities, the natural environment, and society.[4] Eventide Asset Management has recently created the Eventide Center for Faith & Investing because they indeed believe theology is the best basis for picking stocks.[5]

Rather than religion fitting into a secular story, the truth is quite the opposite: all of life and human history fits inside the biblical story. It's a countercultural decision, but people like Robin believe that what's right is also what's smart and that integrating insights from Scripture into their work will ultimately lead to better results for their investors and for the world.

THE DIVINE DRAMA

Theologians like Michael Goheen, the author *The Drama of Scripture*, liken the biblical story to a drama with six acts.

Act 1—The Creation of the World (Genesis 1–2)

Act 2—The Fall and Its Consequences for the World (Genesis 3–12)

Act 3—The Calling of Israel as God's People (Genesis 12—Malachi)

Act 4—The Life, Death and Resurrection of Jesus Christ (Matthew–John)

Act 5—The Calling and Sending of the Church (Acts–Jude)

Act 6—The Judgment and Ultimate Renewal of All Things (Revelation)[6]

Typically, conservative Christians have tended to see the biblical story in light of sin: our fall and God's payment for our sins on the cross. This is, of course, central to the biblical story, but it's too individualistic. It omits God's purposes for all of creation, both the natural world and the systems of the human world (such as health care, government, or business).

Conversely, progressive Christians have tended to see the biblical story in light of justice: God's work to bring his kingdom and bring peace to the here and now. But this can often be too collectivist, overlooking the very personal nature of redemption and God's call for our lives. The six-act gospel sees both: individual salvation and corporate redemption. He has a purpose both for us as individuals and he calls people to bear his name and participate in the healing of the world.

Right now, we are living between Act 5 and Act 6. Christians are sent into the world to love God, serve our neighbors, and demonstrate the gospel with our lives to an unbelieving world. And because work is a very large part of those lives, it is a critical way to carry out God's mission to heal and restore his world.

A good way to begin to think theologically about your work is to take this simple framework and ask critical questions not just about your work but about your company (or school, hospital, etc.) and the industry you work in (see chap. 8). For example,

- What is good about my company or industry that I can support and get behind (creation)?

- What is broken about my company or industry that needs redemption (fall)?

- What might it look like if this part of my company or industry was healed and restored (renewal)?

- What has God put before me today, in my current circumstances, that can be part of that healing and restoration (calling)?

For example, Robin John saw that investing could be an avenue for blessing because business activity itself was a part of providing for the material needs of the world (creation). He also saw businesses could extract value from communities by greed and by practices and products that plunder communities (fall). He then imagined with a group of friends what it might look like to create a mutual fund that invests in businesses "that make the world rejoice" (renewal). Finally, he decided to start a company that would do just that—allocate investor dollars that his team believes contribute to human flourishing by investing in the long-term good of customers, employers, supply chains, host communities, the natural environment, and society at large (calling).

Perhaps you work as a legal assistant for a family law attorney who can see both the goodness of just legal systems and the fallenness of marital conflict, or as a machinist who regularly experiences the satisfaction of producing a well-cut prototype and the pain of a tyrannical boss. The biblical story is a way for us to see our jobs, our work, and our industries.

Theology isn't just for academics. It's for every day, every activity, and every part of the world.

WHEN THEOLOGY HITS THE GROUND RUNNING

Thinking theologically leads to a more whole, human life because we can see the comprehensive picture. It often also leads to innovation.

Take, for example, sales. Realizing that a staggering one in nine people in the American economy work in sales,[7] my former colleague Brian Gray, who works with young professionals in Denver, started to ask his 5280 Fellows (a reference to the Mile High City) bigger questions about their faith and work, and how it might play out in sales. He started with the pain points he was hearing from the young professionals he worked with, which spanned from sticky moral choices to off-kilter industry norms. He asked them to think theologically by asking bigger questions about sales:

- Does this product really matter or add enough good?
- Am I artificially elevating a need to then address it?
- Do I take advantage of information inequity, intentionally hiding from my customer what my product can and can't do?
- Is my number and my sense of worth/identity getting entangled?
- Am I doing what is best for the company, the client, or my commission?

Months later, Brian put together a lunch discussion for Christian professionals working in sales. He then drew on the New Testament's teachings on the kingdom of God to ask even better questions: How do you define success in sales? Who are you as a Christian who sells? What is your Christian responsibility to others in selling? One of his fellows created a professional project titled "Selfless Sales" as a part of her educational experience, and reconfigured the sales incentive structure for herself and other bankers at her credit union. The process began with the assumption that there's something good worth saving (providing a good and needed product), and yet something deeply broken and in need of redemption (selling what primarily serves the salesperson financially). It then moved from imagination to practical action.[8]

In *Creation Regained*, Al Wolters makes the point that Christians are reformers, not revolutionaries. A revolutionary wants to wipe the slate clean and start over, but a reformer seeks to restore something that's been tarnished, acknowledging that it was once good. "Humankind, which has botched its original mandate and the whole creation along with it, is given another chance in Christ; we are reinstated as God's managers on earth," writes Wolters. "The original good creation is to be restored."[9] In the same way, when we carry the truth of Scripture with us into our work, such as in sales, we restore a small part of the world that God so loves (John 3:16).

Thinking theologically means that everything you see—every system, every relationship, every company, every movie, everything—carries with it the weight of sin, the potential for redemption, and the summons to each of us to participate in God's healing of the world.

DOING THE HARD WORK

Reading theologians, studying Scripture, listening to sermons, examining church history, memorizing creeds—this is so much work! Yes, that's 100 percent correct. Thinking theologically is hard, taxing work.

But so is preparing for a final exam, walking alongside a friend going through a divorce, training for a marathon, signing yourself up for an Alcoholics Anonymous group, or working at a job for extra hours to pay for your child's sports fees. Genuine growth is difficult, and work is often hard, but we cannot truly become like Christ without the renewing of our minds (Romans 12:1-2).

We need to learn. We need to think. We need to be reading, listening, and applying. And we need to do so in Christian community, like a church. Worldview is important. Doctrines are tools for seeing reality. And the gospel is not just a private truth; it is the public truth for all things.

Here are some practices I've noticed among those who excel at thinking theologically.

Decide that thinking well is a nonnegotiable part of your Christian life. In the struggle for civil rights, Dr. Martin Luther King Jr. gave a sermon on August 30, 1959, encouraging his listeners to be both tough-minded and tenderhearted. Drawing on Jesus' command to become wise as serpents and innocent as doves, he says being tough-minded "is that quality of life characterized by incisive thinking, realistic appraisal, and decisive judgment. The tough mind is sharp and penetrating. It breaks through the crust of legends and myths, and sifts the true from the false. The tough-minded individual is astute and discerning."

And yet, says Dr. King, "So few people ever achieve it. All too many are content with the soft mind. It is a rarity indeed to find men willing to engage in hard, solid thinking."[10] The majority, says Dr. King, are gullible and willing to accept advertising and political slogans as truth. Few make the real commitment to being both tough-minded and tenderhearted.

Every idea—whether a work email or a storyline in a movie—must be held up to the light of truth. This commitment goes hand in hand with the commitment to following Christ as both Lord and Teacher.

Make space in your schedule and your home for clear thinking. Our world is crowded with noise. Social media, apps, news headlines, emails—finding the quiet space to actually think and reflect has become a real challenge in a world addicted to being connected all the time. We are too busy and constantly distracted.

It takes discipline to shut the screen off and get out a notebook. It takes resolve to refuse the easy media of Netflix and choose the slow media of the written word. It takes forethought to gather a group of friends for a conversation about a substantive book and direct the conversation toward questions that matter.

We must choose to make space for a deeper, broader life. It won't happen by accident.

Choose your reading diet wisely. Tim Macready is from Sydney, Australia. Sporting glasses, goatee, and a down-under accent, Tim's work has led him to the intersection of Christian faith, social justice, environmental stewardship, and business. His work requires him to understand everything from financial projections to international markets.

And yet, when I asked Tim recently about the books that most helped him in his work, he mentioned Dietrich Bonhoeffer's *Life Together* and *The Cost of Discipleship.* Theology, he said, helped him better understand human nature, which directly influenced how he thought of investing, business, and those he works with each day.

People like Tim are intentional with both their reading diet and their friendships. As a result, they become wise (Proverbs 13:20). And they don't read just theology, they read broadly outside their fields. Doing so helps them make connections between topics, including connecting theology to the secular world they live in. Broad reading, broad listening, and broad relationships open the path to seeing a broader slice of God's world.[11]

Take risks based on what you know to be true. Thinking theologically is not just an intellectual activity disconnected from the rest of life. It's a habit that is strengthened through practice, action, and then reflection.

Mary Poplin has spent her career teaching teachers. After a lifetime of reflection on how Christian faith can and should be lived out as a public school teacher, Mary counsels believers in education to take practical action steps based on the Christian worldview.

"Give kids direct instruction," Mary said in a talk she gave to other public school teachers. "Be strict, but have high personal interaction with students and believe in their potential. Teach religion in public schools in a way that's fair. Don't romanticize history—either secular or Christian. Teach virtue and encourage moral conversations among students. Pray for your students. Be courageous in sharing your faith, and compassionate with other views."[12]

Mary believes deeply that thinking well and living well are two sides of the same coin of faithfulness in a secular industry.

Embrace that thinking theologically is for you, no matter your job, community, or title. Thinking theologically is for the rich and the poor, for those with PhDs and those with high school degrees, for those who are culture makers and those who are culture takers.

Take, for example, two very different people: Gisela Kreglinger and Gregorio Trinidad. Gisela is a vintner who grew up on a family winery in Bavaria in southeast Germany. She went on to get a PhD from the University of Edinburgh and write a comprehensive biblical theology of wine in the biblical narrative, titled *The Spirituality of Wine*. A world away, Gregorio is an immigrant to the United States who works in Denver to support family back in Mexico. His family has a small farm in central Mexico that he regularly visits, in which he raises corn for *elote*, grilled corn on the cob covered in mayonnaise, chili powder, lime, and cheese. He once said about his family farm, "Today, on December 2, we sow [seeds] in the name of our Creator and in that same name we hope with faith and patience that by February 20 we can enjoy the fruit of that sowing." Though Gisela and Gregorio are from different social worlds, they both work in agriculture and they both see their work in light of Christian revelation.

THEOLOGICAL ACTION

In December 2019, University of North Carolina professor Molly Worthen wrote an op-ed for the *New York Times* titled, "What Would Jesus Do About Inequality?" She featured leading voices on vocation in the United States, noting that the faith and work movement today is more interested in economic justice than baptizing laissez-faire economics. She also wrote, "In today's evangelicalism, this is where the theological action is: the faith and work movement, the intersection of Christianity with the demands of the workplace and the broader economy."[13] I had to read that twice before pausing to feel a proper sense of pride in being a small part of "where the theological action is." Theology, if we pursue it and know it, is indeed intended for action.

It's easy to dismiss thinking theologically as being important only for the academically minded. This simply isn't true. It is a gift from God for *all* the church to see our work and daily life in light of Scripture, Christian doctrine, and the gospel of grace. The psalmist was right: "In your light, we see light." But to do that, we need to admit that what we think is who we become. "For as he thinks within himself, so he is" (Proverbs 23:7 NASB).

Some of the finest theological insights, I've found, come not from the ivory tower but from people like Dave Lopes, praying and thinking over the sandy gravel of the parking lot.

Embrace Relationships

*The Word became flesh and made his dwelling among us. We
have seen his glory, the glory of the one and only Son, who came
from the Father, full of grace and truth.*

JOHN 1:14

The glass door opens, and a smiling host in a suit and tie
welcomes guests to Canlis, a fine dining restaurant in Seattle. Low
light, crackling fireplace, and white table linens create an air of ele-
gance. Over a hundred servers, cooks, and employees buzz around
with grace and speed to serve guests celebrating special events like
anniversaries, birthdays, or college graduations.

Food & Wine magazine called Canlis "one of the 40 most important restaurants in the past 40 years." Canlis has also been nomi-
nated for fifteen James Beard Awards, which recognize "exceptional
talent and achievement in the culinary arts, hospitality, media, and
the broader food system." They won three.

The secret to their success? "To live out and grow the idea that more
often than not, it's worth putting other people first," says Mark Canlis,
who took over the family business in 2007, alongside his brother. "We've
sought to understand what turning toward one another really looks like
and in so doing, see if our restaurant would stand the test of time."

Having endured since 1950—including surviving a global pandemic that caused the need for fine dining to evaporate in a matter of days—Canlis has indeed stood the test of time because of their focus on relationships with both customers and employees. "Discovering what your employee wants might be the most valuable and precious thing you can do as a business owner," Mark states. The culture embraced by Canlis employees is the secret sauce to their fine dining success.[1]

Relationships are the marrow of workplace culture—relationships between management and employees, employees and fellow employees, and employees and customers. They're the heartbeat of a school or company, and they're also a source of tension, pain, and often why people quit.

One study found the top reasons people quit included lack of recognition, bad managers, poor organizational communication, and unrecognized employee efforts.[2] A *Harvard Business Review* article echoed the same story: people quit principally because of bad management or a lack of appreciation.[3] Interestingly, compensation is always down the list of what keeps people at jobs, but relationships, communication, and workplace culture are always at the top.[4]

Family and work are *the* contexts for the growth—or deterioration—of human relationships. To work well we must embrace relationships, whether we're managers or employees, order-givers or order-takers. But relationships are flat-out hard work, especially in a lonely, individualistic culture built on the myth of personal success. "Love one another as I have first loved you," can be a thorny proposition in the realities of manufacturing, retail, public education, or food service.

Yet for those who worship a God who *is* relationship, learning to live and work alongside other human beings, with all their flaws and quirks, is essential.

HEALTHY RELATIONSHIPS

One of my former coworkers, Lisa Slayton, proudly got a tattoo for her sixtieth birthday. Emblazoned on her ankle is an image representing the Trinity, with three hands each holding a cup, pouring out living water into each other's cups. For Lisa, a former nonprofit CEO and vocational discernment coach, this image of the Trinity is *the* model for healthy relationships.

Secular culture is built around the individual and individual rights, but Christianity is built around the triune God, who is Father, Son, and Holy Spirit. God is distinctly three different persons, yet always connected to the other persons of the Trinity through self-giving love. He is a "divine dance," in the words of Franciscan priest Richard Rohr, into which his people are called to participate (1 Peter 1:4).

Distinct but connected, receiving love yet giving love, self-assured yet self-sacrificial—the Trinity gives us a model for healthy, satisfying relationships.

One way to think about healthy relationships is the ability to "differentiate" yourself yet stay connected to others. Edwin Freidman, a rabbi, family therapist, leadership consultant, and author, writes,

> Differentiation means the capacity of a family member to define his or her own life's goals and values apart from surrounding togetherness pressures, to say "I" when others are demanding "you" and "we." It includes the capacity to maintain a (relatively) nonanxious presence in the midst of anxious systems, to take maximal responsibility for one's own destiny and emotional well-being. . . . The concept should not be confused with autonomy or narcissism, however. Differentiation means the capacity to be an "I" while remaining connected.[5]

Murray Bowen, an American psychiatrist and founder of family systems theory, proposed a scale of differentiation. On one side is enmeshment, being completely lost in another and letting that person command your sense of well-being and identity. On the other side is detachment and being emotionally cutoff from relationships. Health is in the middle: balancing individual autonomy with to-getherness or intimacy. It is staying in relationship with others while being very clear about one's own beliefs and values.[6]

In the Gospels, we see Christ living out this kind of balanced differentiation. He was in relationship with his twelve disciples, yet he also sought solitude to pray. Jesus had a crystal-clear understanding of his convictions, values, and purpose. Staying true to these, he challenged the Pharisees, and, when necessary, his closest friends, like Peter. As Christ hung on the cross, he did this perfectly, staying connected to his mother and John, yet unwavering in his commitment to God's plan of salvation. He is distinct from those around him yet intimately connected to his followers.

Practically speaking, the test for our relationships comes when we face a crisis. When a child throws a spoon at us in anger at the dinner table and we feel the blood rushing to our head, how will we respond? (I'm speaking hypothetically, of course!) Or when your boss disciplines you for not completing a project on time that you did not have the authority or budget to complete, and your heart begins to race, how will you respond?

Tracy Mathews, the founder of Attune, says, "Maturity is the ability to maintain a relational state under pressure."[7] That is, when you feel a surge of rage or stress behind your eyes, can you calmly state your perspective and allow the other person to share theirs? Or do you flee, fight, or freeze?

Taking responsibility for your own emotions, refusing to negate or write others off, and responding with clarity, conviction and connectedness in a moment of stress is the test of the emotionally mature individual.

SELF-AWARENESS AND
RELATIONAL INTELLIGENCE

Unfortunately, for most of my career, I've been the very opposite of an emotionally mature individual. In conversations with donors and coworkers, I've let my excitement for ideas run roughshod over people, cutting them off mid-sentence. In one meeting, when things didn't go my way, I slumped back in my chair, folded my arms and just about broadcast with a megaphone, "I didn't like that and now I'm disengaging!" In another meeting, I showed up with plans so buttoned up and airtight, it was as if I was telling my incredibly bright, competent coworkers, "Your feedback isn't necessary. Just do as I say and all will be well with you!" In short, I've lacked both self-awareness and relational intelligence.

The good news is that we can change. We're not static, and there is an abundance of tools to help us grow in emotional maturity and self-awareness. Enneagram, DISC Assessment, Strengths Finder, Myers-Briggs, 360-degree peer reviews, and EQi Assessment are just a few that can help us grow. One assessment that has been particularly helpful to me is the SIMA—System for Identifying Motivated Abilities. As the former leader of a non-profit, I had the privilege of having a coach walk me through my most motivating environments and roles, my natural abilities, the results I look for, and the upsides and downsides of my personality. Another tool for growing in emotional health and self-awareness is Steve Cuss's Capable Life membership, a community that helps people identify and manage anxiety in the home and work.[8]

One tool to help employees grow in working well with coworkers is the "User Guide."[9] Employees complete a simple questionnaire, which helps coworkers understand how to work with them, similar to a user guide for a machine or tech tool. Questions include:

- My Personality and Quirks: Are you an introvert or extrovert? What's your Enneagram number or Myers-Briggs? What quirks have your spouse or a roommate told you about?

- How to Best Communicate with Me: What's my verbal communication style? How far in advance do I prefer to get requests for tasks? Do I prefer verbal, text, Slack, or email?

- How I Give and Receive Feedback: What's the best way to give me feedback? What's the best time or setting? How do I respond to feedback—at my best and my worst? How do I offer feedback to others—at my best and my worst?

Tools like this have given me more than one "eureka!" moment with my coworkers, particularly when listening to how others answer these questions. The investment in self-awareness is ultimately an investment in relationships. And 100 percent of organizations are made or unmade based on whether or not people can work together for a common purpose.

Healthy organizational culture is not formed by values written on a wall but instead by people with healthy relationships who know themselves and one another.

CONFLICT AND RECONCILIATION

Healthy relationships are hard work. Conflict is the norm for most relationships, not harmony.

Shannon Allen and Rachel Anderson would know. As divorce attorneys, they have seen the worst in relational conflict: custody battles, bitter name calling, and ugly, expensive lawsuits in court that result in a lose-lose situation, with children often being the biggest losers. "Relational conflict is hard," they write. "Facing it is uncomfortable. Experiencing conflict affects our daily rhythms and routines. Conflict can even cause us to doubt God's goodness, His will for our lives, or His love for us. But, in fact, God often uses conflict to refine our character and draw us closer to him."

As Christians in law, Rachel and Shannon creatively imagined what being divorce attorneys might look like in light of their faith. They lay out several principles for their work with couples that equally apply to workplace relationships and marriages. First, begin the reconciliation process with self-reflection, recognizing that each of us have sinned and fallen short of God's glory (Romans 3:23; Matthew 7:3-5). Second, rather than avoiding conflict, initiate reconciliation and take the first step toward peace. Ask for forgiveness for your side of the issue before a conflict grows (Matthew 5:23-24, 18:15; Galatians 6:1). Third, if necessary, invite an intermediary to help when emotions run high. For coworkers, this could be asking for help from a manager or the HR department, ideally somebody who shares your faith (1 Corinthians 6:1-8).[10]

Other times, you might be called to bring reconciliation between clients, teachers, patients, or coworkers. This has been the task for much of the career of Stephanie Summers, the CEO at the Center for Public Justice, an independent, nonpartisan organization based in Washington, DC, that seeks to "help citizens and public office holders respond to God's call to do justice." Because Christians, too, often clash with one another on perspective in politics and public life, Stephanie has developed a process to find common ground between conservatives and progressives.

When working to solve thorny disputes between diverse perspectives, Stephanie believes you need to get to know your collaborators, define principles on which people agree, listen to understand, and name differences. "We are trusting that God can work with people who may not know him as Lord and Savior." She works with people from all faiths—or no faith—as she notes, "I take you seriously as a human, and recognize that God is at work in our work."

The reason we treat all people—even those with whom we disagree with on politics—as human is because they are first reflections of God himself.[11]

Conflict will come to all of us, but those who openly address it, embrace it as a normal part of healthy relationships, and believe God uses it to refine character, are those who lead in their companies, communities, and industries.

They also end up with the hardened gem of healthy, fulfilling relationships.

WORK AND FAMILY

It was February 26, 2015, and it began to snow.

Joanna Meyer, my former colleague at Denver Institute, and I were finishing setting up chairs at Palazzo Verdi, a high-end event venue. It was complete with a purple, spiral chandelier hanging from the ceiling, citrus-infused water for guests, and chocolate-covered strawberries.

As the snow turned into a blizzard, we wondered if anybody would come. But in less than an hour, 250 women braved a blizzard for an event we called "Women, Work & Calling."

Here's how Joanna described the gathering: "Whether women are working at home, professionally, in the wider community or all of the above, they face unique challenges as they seek to faithfully navigate the complexity of their calling. For Christians seeking to steward the fullness of their lives, finding better language and more flexible frameworks to think about the many dimensions of a woman's work is essential. In the midst of inevitable tensions and uncertainties, how does our faith address the questions many women face, and how can the church better equip women in their vocation?"

Joanna and her team had hit a nerve. Women across the city struggled with questions about work, family, calling, and influence. Not just women, but men (like myself) also struggle deeply with how to invest in work relationships and family relationships, often being pulled in opposite directions.

Since that evening in 2015, the conversation around women, family, and work has continued to grow. Sheryl Sandberg wrote the bestselling book *Lean In,* Anne-Marie Slaughter stirred the pot with an essay in the *Atlantic* "Why Women Still Can't Have It All," and when schools and childcare centers closed down, the Covid-19 pandemic cause 3.5 million American mothers to leave the workforce. As of mid-2022, most hadn't returned.[12] The tensions workers face between family and the job are real and growing.

Though these questions can't be easily answered, there are faithful responses. Kate Harris, mother of four and author of *Wonder Women: Navigating the Challenges of Motherhood, Career and Identity,* believes calling—and the tensions between work and family relationships—can best be understood in three ways. Calling is comprehensive, involves constraint, and requires consent.

Kate believes God's call is *comprehensive* in that we serve him just as much at work as we do in our family. It touches all arenas of life. Whether we're driving kids to soccer or driving the bottom line, it's all part of a life lived in response to God's voice. Second, Jesus himself was incarnate, meaning he lived under the *constraint* of a single body, with a particular set of disciples, in one place. He didn't do everything and go everywhere, and he doesn't expect us to either. Our limitations are part of God's good plan, not hindrances to a "life of impact." Third, God is inviting us to *consent* to our real-life circumstances, whether we're driving a truck to a job site or a son to football practice, whether we're married or single. God invites us to experience him in this moment, right here, right now.[13]

Rather than living in the anxiety-driven tensions that pit family and work priorities against one another, God calls us to offer life to him in the present. As Jean-Pierre de Caussade writes, we're called to offer our souls "light as a feather, fluid as water, innocent as a child" to God as if we were responding to "to every movement of grace like a floating balloon."[14]

Each moment of the day, whether with coworkers or kids, is lived from a single, comprehensive calling to respond to God's voice in all areas of life.

Professional Versus Working-Class Perspectives

Networks Versus "Real Work"
Many professional jobs involve social skills and managing networks of influence. Yet the working class feel that their work, which often involves technical expertise, is more down-to-earth than the work of professionals, and more practically valuable.

Many in the working class also feel a deep sense of pride in their work.[15] Matthew Crawford, author of "Shop Class as Soulcraft," points out the dignity the manual laborer feels after a day's work. "He can simply point: the building stands, the car now runs, the lights are on."[16] One values relational influence, the other tends to value practical usefulness. Also, professionals tend to value work-related success more highly. The working class tends to value family and friendship more.

Each can learn from the other. In a culture where social capital (networks of relationships) is declining for working-class communities, professionals can help their working-class coworkers by inviting them into networks, introducing them to friends, and opening doors of opportunity.[17] Conversely, in a culture obsessed with individual success, working-class men and women can help their professional coworkers see the value in friendship and family as intrinsic goods apart from never-ending productivity. They can also introduce professionals to the physical world, filled with products of human work like landscaping, electrical conduit, clean hotel rooms, warehouses, call centers, and concrete sidewalks.

EMBRACE RELATIONSHIPS

It is no small task to embrace relationships. They require real work, and, in the short-term, it's far easier to escape or write people off. But all the research points to the same conclusion: those who have meaningful lives invest their time, money, and resources into good relationships.[18]

Here are a few ways to begin cultivating healthy relationships.

Commit to face-to-face meetings. Covid-19 caused a large-scale shift to remote work. But, if you can, push back. Working primarily through screens can be efficient and often convenient, but it's not very human. When you meet in person with somebody, you can't secretly scroll social media. You can also pick up on voice tonality, gestures, and other nonverbal cues, which comprise over 90 percent of human communication.

It's not a coincidence that Jesus was God with us. He didn't send his word and messages only through the prophets. He arranged a face-to-face meeting. There's certainly a case to be made for the flexible work schedules that technology affords us, especially to accommodate family needs. But we are made for in-the-flesh interaction, and when we can, we should find ways to meet friends, family members, clients, and coworkers face-to-face.

Take a leader out to coffee. Reading books is one way to learn. A far better and lasting way is to reach out to somebody you admire and buy them coffee or invite them to share a meal. The number one predictor of career success is having broad professional networks.[19] The reason is that people who know others from different job functions, backgrounds, or industries become valuable connectors between different social groups. Also, exposure to people with very different experiences broadens your horizons and skill sets.

Making the time to do this is tough for most of us. But investing in good relationships will pay dividends.

Commit to long-term relationships. Imagine if you came home from work and said to your spouse, "I need food now." Your spouse places food at your table, and you leave dirty dishes without so much as a hello. After an hour, your spouse calls a friend and confesses, "It's fine. All I really need from my spouse is a paycheck anyway."

You would never do this because spouses are not there to be used but to be loved. Nevertheless, this is sometimes how we treat coworkers, customers, or bosses. We stay in relationships as long as we benefit personally, with money being the artificial glue holding together many workplaces.

Instead, be countercultural. Take a former employee out for breakfast two months after he quit, just to check in. Call up a boss you had ten years ago to say thanks for teaching you that valuable lesson early in your career. Remember the name of the guy who serves you coffee each day at Dunkin' Donuts. Write a note of appreciation to a coworker.

People are not a means to an end—they *are the end in themselves.* Commit to long-term relationships with people you work with because people have intrinsic value, apart from whether they can help you get ahead or not.

Invest in your company's culture. The best places to work value employee input (and ask for it regularly). They empower employees to make decisions and help them learn and grow, have fun on the job, and create a sense of family and togetherness on their team.[20] For this to happen, somebody has to rise up from the day-to-day tasks, take initiative, and decide that it's worth the time and effort to build healthy workplace relationships.

Ultimately, the culture of your company will shape you. But will you go out of your way to shape it?

Pay attention. We live in a deeply disconnected, distracted age. Screens, media, and noise are everywhere. Because of our culture, oftentimes the deepest generosity we can offer others is attention.

Pay attention to what somebody is saying. Shut off your phone and make eye contact. Ask questions that require active listening. Be sensitive to others' nonverbal cues. Take note when a fellow teacher says he loves black tea, not black coffee.

Mark Stevenson, an executive coach, once asked me a pointed question: "What does it look like when you love somebody?" As a distracted guy with thousands of ideas, I immediately thought of my wife and daughters and I said, "Oh, it's when I pay attention to them. Deeply, intently, and without distraction."

SERVING TABLES

The temptation in our relationships—especially hard ones—is to "fix" the other person, as if this would magically make life easier.

But Mark Canlis, the restaurant owner in Seattle, knows better. Mark said of his employees, "It's not my job to change them. That's the Spirit's work. Our job is to be living lives that would pique their curiosity around change. You open the door for the Holy Spirit to move through."

"The operative conversation," Mark says, "is who are you becoming?"

6

Create Good Work

I planted the seed, Apollos watered it, but God has been making
it grow. So neither the one who plants nor the one who waters
is anything, but only God, who makes things grow. . . . For we
are coworkers in God's service.

1 CORINTHIANS 3:6-7, 9

Josh Mabe led me behind his shop. "It's a mess back here," he said. What I saw was not your typical Home Depot fare. There were old railroad carts, wine barrels, deserted barn doors, discarded flooring from nineteenth-century homes, planks from the bed of a semi-truck trailer. Each piece had a common theme: it had been abandoned by somebody else.

But for Mabe, each piece of discarded lumber is the object of his craft, an opportunity to bring life from decay. Josh is the owner of Twenty1Five, a small furniture business specializing in reclaimed wood located in Palmer Lake, Colorado, nestled at the foot of the Rocky Mountains. Josh, a carpenter and craftsman, has attracted statewide attention. Rocky Mountain PBS, *5280 Home*, and *Luxe* magazine have praised his attention to sustainability and "upcycling"—creating new products from used materials.

Yet it's the products themselves that turn heads. His tables are mosaics of shapes, textures, and colors. He can turn drab boardrooms into a collage of natural beauty, and sterile kitchens into a wild array of Mountain West history.

"I've always enjoyed working with my hands," Mabe recalls. After college he taught shop class for eleven years at a public school. A retired coworker would leave scrap wood behind the school—"what people would consider ugly wood." But Mabe, unable to part with the discarded lumber, took it home and built a table for his wife from the "reclaimed" wood. The table caught the attention of his neighbors, though initially nothing came of it.

For financial reasons, Mabe took a job selling insurance. "But I was dying on the vine," he told his wife, lamenting the confines of an office. "That day," Mabe recalls, "I distinctly remember God telling me, 'Go, make tables. And in two weeks I'll bring you orders.'" That Monday, he went to his shop and began to build. Orders came in. Word began to spread, and his new business was born.[1]

THORNY WORK

Mabe's story reminds me that our daily work is filled with hope and pain, dreams and setbacks, accomplishments and struggles. Each day, as we care for patients, teach students, fix homes, and listen to customers, we are caught between the beauty of cultivating God's good world and beating back the thorns and thistles of a fallen creation (Genesis 2:15; 3:17-18). Sometimes the orders for tables come in; sometimes they don't.

The thorns of work in our culture seem to be multiplying. First, we tend to either overvalue or undervalue our work. Most professionals have made work their religion, seeing work as the source of identity, self-worth, and impact in the world. The religion of "workism" is indeed making professionals miserable.[2]

Yet on the other side of the economy, people disengage from work, seeing it as nothing more than a necessary evil. Millions of working-age men have dropped out of the workforce completely, opting for entertainment and disability benefits rather than jobs, families, and homes.[3] Gallup reports that about 15 percent of all Americans are actively disengaged from their jobs.[4] Most, I'd venture, at least since the pandemic, have felt the slow creep of *acedia* or sloth in our work, languishing in the long afternoon sun of infinite tasks yet finite energy.[5] Work can feel like an exhausting marathon, which we will only be saved from at retirement.[6]

Second, work is distracting. The advent of the internet and smartphones have affected all corners of creation. Attention spans have become even shorter, and anxiety is on the rise.[7] But it wasn't always this way. The Shakers had an interesting philosophy of furniture making. "Make every product better than it's ever been done before. Make the parts you cannot see as well as the parts you can see. Use only the best materials, even for the most everyday items. Give the same attention to the smallest detail as you do to the largest. Design every item you make to last forever."[8] Though this philosophy is beautiful, with little red notifications buzzing in our pockets every few minutes, doing quality, lasting work is nearly a herculean effort. Distraction is the norm in a digital age.

Third, millions are underpaid and underappreciated for the work they do. In July 2022 Just Capital did a survey of the issues American workers care most about. Far and away the most important issue to American workers isn't communities, climate change, or corporate governance; it is "pays a fair living wage."[9] In the fall of 2022, support for unions was at its highest since the 1960s. It's no wonder. At a time of deep divisions, Blacks, Hispanics, Whites, Republicans, Democrats, women, those over and under age sixty-five can all agree that they want to be respected for their work and compensated fairly.[10]

Yet, despite undervaluing or overvaluing work, the distractions we face, and the wide underappreciation and undercompensation, we sense that work is part of a whole, meaningful life. Not only do we spend nearly ninety thousand hours at work throughout life, but we look to it for a sense of purpose.[11] In the 1970s journalist Studs Turkel wrote, "Work is about a search for daily meaning as well as daily bread, for recognition as well as cash, for astonishment rather than torpor; in short, for a sort of life rather than a Monday-through-Friday sort of dying."[12] We long to be seen. We long for our work to be remembered. We long for fulfillment and meaning.

If we want to live a full, happy life, we'll have to find ladders to climb out of this damp, dark hole we've found ourselves in. To do that, we first need to reestablish the value of work itself.

WHEN FIRES BURN THEMSELVES OUT

"Daddy, what if there were no stores?" That was the question my then four-year-old daughter asked on the way home from church. As we cruised down South Santa Fe in south Denver, perhaps she noticed the German Auto Parts Dealer and wondered what took place within those four walls, or the fact that St. Nick's Christmas and Collectibles was closed for the season. Either way, it was an interesting question.

"Well, Sierra, just imagine," I replied, looking at a gas station, then a shopping mall. "If there were no stores, we wouldn't have this car we're driving in. We couldn't be driving on roads, these street lights wouldn't work at night, and we wouldn't have these clothes on our backs. We'd be naked!" She giggled in the back seat. "We wouldn't have any food in the grocery stores, our house would eventually fall apart, and we wouldn't have any warm baths."

"And dad, there wouldn't be any doctors!" she replied. This was of great concern to her because pretending to be a doctor was one of her favorite games. "Nope, no doctors," I said. "Wouldn't that be terrible?"[13]

My daughter's question reminded me of a book written by Lester DeKoster, a lifelong librarian. "Imagine that everyone quits working, right now! What happens? Civilized life quickly melts away," DeKoster writes in *Work: The Meaning of Your Life*. "Food vanishes from store shelves, gas pumps dry up, streets are no longer patrolled, and fires burn themselves out. Communication and transportation services end and utilities go dead. Those who survive at all are soon huddled around campfires, sleeping in tents, and clothed in rags."

This dystopian scene reminds us of an important truth: work is meaningful because it is the form in which we make ourselves useful to others.[14] Indeed, work is not just the way we make civilization; it is how we contribute to the great symphony we call the modern economy.

Yet good work is also a key ingredient in a happy life. Charles Murray, an author and researcher at the American Enterprise Institute, found that people who are unmarried, dissatisfied with their work, professing no religion, and have low social trust had only a 10 percent chance of saying they're "very happy" with their life. Having either a happy marriage or a satisfying job increased that number to 19 percent. But for those who have both a very satisfying job and a very satisfying marriage, the number jumps to 55 percent. Having high social trust bumps the number to 69 percent, and if you add in strong religious involvement, its raises even further to 76 percent. Stunningly, for his sample set—Whites from ages thirty to forty-nine—having all four elements (happy marriage, high social trust, religious involvement, and a satisfying job) closes the gap of self-reported happiness between those with high incomes and those with low incomes.[15] Good work alone won't make you happy, but it is one of the key ingredients to being happy with your life.

We might pause here to say that there are many who don't work and are completely happy. And yet, if we think of work broadly as both paid and unpaid labor, we find that students, volunteers, stay-at-home parents, and retirees who are engaged in committed service to others are consistently happier than those whose lives revolve around self-focused pleasure or idleness. John Stott, the late great Anglican author and leader, defined work simply as "the expenditure of energy (manual or mental or both) *in the service of others*, which brings fulfillment to the worker, benefit to the community, and glory to God."[16]

Getting a paycheck is, indeed, important, but what gives us spiritual satisfaction from work is the opportunity to use our talents to love our neighbors as ourselves.

BREATH OF LIFE

Work can indeed be a drag. But work can also breathe life into communities. Work, I've noticed, has a particular power when motivated by the biblical story, rather than success or money. Four doctrines can breathe new life into our work: the doctrine of creation, the priesthood of all believers, the resurrection, and the stewardship of our gifts.

The doctrine of creation. Dave Hataj grew up with a dad who struggled with alcoholism. His alcoholism seeped into the family business, a small manufacturing company in Wisconsin. Remembering parties at the office and pornography on the walls, he recounts, "By the time I was 18, I knew something was very, very wrong. Something felt dark." Depressed and drinking heavily, Hataj turned to running as an escape. One day on a long run through country roads, "I remember a voice coming to me. I said, 'Who's playing a trick on me?' I just remember this voice saying, 'You are not alone. I've been with you through all of it.'" To Dave, the message was clear: God had been with him through all of his life's struggles.

Dave realized for the first time that he was not an accident and that his life had purpose.

Today, Hataj is the second-generation owner of Edgerton Gear, a company that makes gears, which in turn make cardboard boxes, aluminum cans, food processing machines, and other everyday items. Dave felt that God was calling him to redeem the culture of his family business. After his conversion, Dave had his work cut out for him to introduce openness, trust, and accountability into the company. A part of the solution was to hire young men of character.

And it made an impact. "When I started working here," says Clayton Flood, a journeyman machinist at Edgerton Gear, "I was nervous. It'll probably be hardy, tough guys. But it was super nice people. Boss really cares for me here, and that's why I felt comfortable becoming a machinist." In a similar vein, "This is an actually happy environment," says Andy Hagen, an apprentice machinist. "You feel like you can talk to your actual coworkers."[17] Culture started to change around character.

Another strategy Hataj used was giving young craftsmen a sense of purpose. He found that many of the young men they were hiring hadn't taken the college route and had taken on an identity of being a failure or "D student." Hataj, however, believes that every person is created to create (Genesis 2:15) and each has God-given talents and skills that their community needs. Hataj has written "The Craftsmen Code" for his employees, which he has new employees memorize. It states:

1. I am not the center of the universe.

2. I do not know everything, nor nearly as much as I think I do.

3. There is dignity and purpose in knowing my trade.

4. The world needs me.

5. Pay is a reward for my efforts, but not my main motivation.

6. Every person has unique gifts and talents.[18]

Dave's renewal of the trades at Edgerton Gear is based on the doctrine that God himself creates, and we too are called to create what the world needs through our work. Or as Dorothy Sayers writes, "Work should be the full expression of the worker's faculties, the thing in which he finds spiritual, mental and bodily satisfaction, and the medium in which he offers himself to God."[19]

The priesthood of all believers. Lesya and Nicholai Login live in the small town of Khust, nestled in the western mountains of Ukraine. They both have a lifelong love of biking, and dreamed of sharing their love of the outdoors with others. As Lesya worked as a teacher and Nicholai as a bike repairman, they hoped to open their own business. But they were consistently rejected for a small business loan because of their age and inexperience.

A neighbor told them about HOPE International, an international microfinance institution. With their first loan from HOPE Ukraine, they bought a few bicycles and began to rent them out. It was a time of spiritual growth as well. Nicholai had shared his faith with Lesya years earlier and they both began attending Nicholai's church. Their story of entrepreneurship and faith was bound together. "Choosing to take the loan was pivotal for me," Lesya says. "I was full of excitement to have my dream come true—that our passion would become our work."

Years later their business grew. They expanded to two locations, a retail brand, and several employees. Not only do they sell bikes and accessories but they also believe their work is a platform for living and sharing their faith. "When God gives, we are called to give back," says Lesya. Working with their local church, they organize an annual bike ride for children. They have also created a youth bicycle club, giving them a positive alternative to alcohol or drugs through the power of community.[20]

The apostle Peter famously wrote, "But you are a chosen people, a royal priesthood, a holy nation, God's special possession, that you may declare the praises of him who called you out of darkness into his wonderful light" (1 Peter 2:9). Peter got the idea of a "royal priesthood" from Exodus 19, when God said to the Israelites, just before giving the Ten Commandments, "Out of all nations you will be my treasured possession. Although the whole earth is mine, you will be for me a kingdom of priests and a holy nation" (Exodus 19:5-6). The role of a priest was to intercede on behalf of the people and mediate God's presence. When God calls his people priests, he intends to make himself known to the world through all of his people, not just clergy. And that can and should take place every day and everywhere, even at a bike shop in a small town in Ukraine.[21]

The resurrection. A longtime friend, Dan Reed, has been a lifelong fundraiser. With short hair, beard, and a quiet attentiveness in any conversation, Dan is the founder of Seed Fundraisers, a coaching organization that trains "elite fundraisers." His passion for fundraising came from years of raising money for the Morris Animal Foundation and seeing his peers in the industry. "Organizations that raise money aren't necessarily the ones solving problems," Dan says. "Organizations solving problems aren't necessarily raising money. And organizations receiving praise are not necessarily healthy places to work." The nonprofit industry, noble as it seems from the outside, is filled with brokenness too.[22]

Fundraisers, says Dan, are often seen instrumentally, meaning that leadership and boards often functionally say to them, "You go find us money so we can do the really important work." And relationships with donors were often just as broken. Fundraisers would either "manage" donors to hit their revenue goals, or they would take on a subservient posture toward donors, bowing to an unhealthy power dynamic. But what if fundraising itself was intrinsically valuable work, apart from the causes it supports, simply because it inspires generosity and hence was a reflection of faith? Dan set out to look for the gold standard in nonprofit fundraising practices. He found that the best fundraisers were more concerned about activating generosity than raising money.

Dan's career was shaped by his understanding of vocation, which, for him, meant that his work had intrinsic value on a daily basis apart from the impact it made. It had value because work itself is a participation in the new creation.

Paul writes, "If anyone is in Christ he is a new creation. The old has gone; the new has come" (2 Corinthians 5:9). The Jews of Jesus' day didn't expect a resurrection of the dead, but they thought it would happen at the end of time when Israel would be restored and a new, earthly Davidic kingdom would come. When Jesus was raised from the dead, there was confusion. After the resurrection, they fully expected an earthly restoration of the Messiah's rule (Acts 1:6). Instead the key event of the end of time—the resurrection—had happened now in the middle of time. Theologians called this the "inaugurated kingdom," or as one Anglican liturgy puts it "the Lamb who was slain has begun his reign." The new heavens and earth are not just a future reality; they have already begun, right here, right now. Even for a fundraiser.

New Testament scholar N. T. Wright puts it succinctly, "Jesus's resurrection is the beginning of God's new project to not snatch people away from earth to heaven but to colonize earth with the life of heaven. That, after all, is what the Lord's prayer is all about."[23]

When Dan Reed looks intently into how and why he does his work as a Christian, he's asking the right question as a person of faith: Since Jesus is raised from the dead and now reigns, how should I live and do my work?

Stewardship of our gifts. Meagan McCoy Jones grew up in the family business. McCoy's Building Supply is a supplier of lumber, building materials, roofing supplies, and farm and ranch equipment in Texas, New Mexico, and Oklahoma. As a teenager, she witnessed her parents have significant conflicts. They worked through marital challenges with the help of a counselor, and the process ultimately influenced Meagan's own leadership of the company decades later. "They became committed to being relationally different, which is incredibly powerful," Meagan recalls about her parents after their marriage crisis.

As a result, the McCoy family brought tools for building healthy relationships into the leadership of their company, which transformed their work at McCoy's. "Our leadership training includes tools like conflict resolution, which is a cute term until you have two super-angry people." Meagan describes how she sees leadership: "Me more deeply knowing you, and then caring about you. The next time I walk in, and I see your project as deserving of both praise and probably some constructive criticism, I'm going to make sure I'm very specific, and make sure to mention both the really good things and things I wish were different."

Today, Meagan believes healthy conflict resolution is critical to a healthy workplace. "I have told my team that if there is any conflict among us, the only work of the day is to resolve the conflict between us."[24]

Generally, when Christians talk about stewarding our gifts, we think about using our skills and talents for God's purpose (1 Peter 4:10). Yet we rarely think about stewarding our pain and suffering as a form of God's grace. Meagan and her parents turned painful family memories into a healthy, redemptive workplace culture because, in part, they believed that even their difficult circumstances were gifts to be stewarded.

We're called to see our talents and our pain, our skills and our suffering, our experiences and our frailty, as one mysterious gift to steward on behalf of those we serve.

"For some reason," says Meagan, "we were given a lumberyard chain. And that's our universe to care about and steward."

Professional Versus Working-Class Perspectives

Discernment Versus Discipline

For professionals, the spiritual and occupational challenge of work is discernment. There are so many good things they could do with their lives—how do they choose?

But for the working class, endless choice isn't a luxury they often have. Instead, getting and keeping a good job through discipline and moral integrity is the higher (and sometimes only) priority. Joan Williams, who researches the opinions of American working-class families, has found that working-class men and women consistently value honesty, integrity, and hard work. "Hard work for elites is associated with self-actualization; 'disruption' means founding a start-up," writes Williams. "Disruption, in working-class jobs, just gets you fired."

Gordon Marino, a college teacher in Northfield, Minnesota, shares the story of students who came into his office "rubbing their hands together, and furrowing their brows, wondering if they should become doctors, philosophers, or stand-up comics, while many people in Northfield deliver papers at 5 a.m. or became roofers. Marino's own father worried very little if he'd 'love his job.' Instead, he worked a job he disliked for most of his career to take care of his family. Responsibility trumped personal desire."[25]

The late Eugene Peterson says something similar, "Not many people have the opportunity to do a job that fits them." Peterson's own dad was a butcher, who, though he didn't particularly enjoy his job, did draw self-respect from it. Peterson remembered his dad having contempt for those "who just wanted to get through the day as fast as they could." The discipline to do a job well done, even an unpleasant job, is key to a working-class view of work.[26]

For the working class, discipline and endurance may be the only way to get a job, advance in a career, and find your way out of the maze. For hourly workers, it's also the way to get your kids out of the maze.

SABBATH: SETTING LIMITS TO OUR WORK

Work was created as good, but to stay good, it needs limits. After years of trial and error, I believe that practicing sabbath is the central practice in healing our relationship with work. "Observe the Sabbath day, to keep it holy. Work six days and do everything you need to do," says the fourth commandment. "But the seventh day is a Sabbath to God, your God. Don't do any work. . . . For in six days God made Heaven, Earth, and sea, and everything in them; he rested on the seventh day. Therefore, God blessed the Sabbath day, he set it apart as a holy day" (Exodus 20:8-11 MSG). Even God, who delighted in his work of creation—and cannot ever be tired—practiced one day of rest out of seven. Sabbath is the key to restoring not only our relationship to work but to our hearts, our communities, and God himself.

In an overly busy, technologically driven world, practicing sabbath has become a challenge. Dr. Ryan Tafilowski, professor of theology at Denver Seminary, lays out three key questions in a free resource called "Deep Rest: A Study on Sabbath."[27]

1. *What will you say no to?* Sabbath is about setting limits. Will you say no to technology for a day a week? What other work demands do you need to refuse on sabbath? What about non-work demands that take as much time on the weekend, like weekend-long hiking trips (if you live in Colorado) or never-ending kid's activities (if you have a family)?

2. *What will you say yes to?* Sabbath is not only about restriction; it is about freedom. Freedom from the tyranny of never-ending demands on our time. What activities restore connection to God, others, creation, and your own sense of peace? Taking a long time to cook a big meal? Taking a long walk in the park? A nap? A book? What do you actually imagine doing when you hear the words, "Come to me, all you who are wearied and burdened, and I will give you rest?" (Matthew 11:28-30).

3. *What sabbath rhythms will you build?* What do you need to do to prepare well for sabbath rest? What kind of rhythm will kick off your sabbath? What kind of family rhythms do you need to reconsider so that all of you can practice sabbath together? What commitments need to be made, and who needs to know about it?

Sabbath recenters our identity as God's children, not endless producers; sabbath recenters our hearts on worshiping God, not the work of our own hands. And sabbath recenters our lives on justice, slowing us down and giving us eyes to see the lost, the lonely, and the overlooked.[28]

Sabbath not only renews our work; it renews our world from the inside out.

KNOTTED BEAUTY

Christian faith offers a real gift to all of us who work. It offers a sense of dignity despite the pain and humiliation our jobs may produce. It offers a rebalancing of the role of work in our lives, avoiding the twin pitfalls of work as meaningless toil and work as everything. It offers a higher vision of work, as a way to serve our neighbors, contribute to God's kingdom each day, and steward our gifts. It provides a humbler vision of our jobs, as it is God ultimately who is the one working in and through us (Philippians 2:3).

And Christian faith too hints at a mystery: that God himself is building a heavenly city, and, by his grace, including human work as the foundation and edifice of his heavenly city (1 Corinthians 3). Though it will be tested and one day purified, he chooses the work of everyday people to adorn his new world (Isaiah 65).

Josh Mabe, sensing this truth, named his small carpentry business Twenty1Five, which is from Revelation 21:5 (NKJV), where Jesus says, "Behold, I make all things new." Their name piques curiosity with both Christian and nonbelieving clients. Yet he tells the story faithfully just the same.

Josh does the work of a laborer. He travels to abandoned barns, weary homesteads, and to the forgotten corners of rural Colorado. He works with customers to "source" each piece of discarded lumber, ultimately to be refashioned into a dining room table, door, or TV stand. He often tells customers the history of each piece of furniture he crafts in his shop—the lifespan of lumber that served, was forgotten, and finally was renewed. And in so doing he shares a subtle tale of redemption—of buying back the useless, of uncovering hidden value.

Thinking back to the advent of his business, Mabe recalls, "What really spurred us on was the story that parallels our lives and what we do. Most of this stuff," pointing to a knotted board in the back of his shop, "is beat up and has got scars, and is discarded lumber. But if you take that stuff and see beyond some of those scars, you can make something really beautiful out of it."

7

Serve
Others Sacrificially

And if anyone gives even a cup of cold water to one of these little ones who is my disciple, truly I tell you, that person will not lose their reward.

MATTHEW 10:42

"**I shouldn't even be alive** for all I did. God had a plan for me, though."

In 2014, Dave Collins, fifty-seven, hit a low point in his battle with alcohol abuse. He lost his job, and then his home, and eventually checked in to the Denver Rescue Mission. The rescue mission's work therapy program introduced him to a second chance and a new job.

Dave is a housekeeper at a six-hundred-room hotel next to the Colorado Convention Center. "Everything I've gone through has been to make me who I am and put me here to serve others," Dave says. His job is to answer calls, keep the lobby clean, and clean rooms. And yet, Dave believes his vocation is ultimately one of hospitality: "I feel like I'm a doorway to show our guests how much they're appreciated."

Social workers, teachers, police officers, and counselors tend to find meaning in their work rather easily; it can be harder for those scrubbing toilets and stocking toiletries. Yet for Dave meaning isn't found in prestige or high wages. He finds value in the daily chance to serve others sacrificially.

Cleaning hotels can be dirty work. Dave has served rooms packed with extra sleepers, intoxicated partiers, and everything in between. Dave recalls one day that a guest got food poisoning and created a mess. But Dave saw another's vulnerability as an opportunity. "I changed her sheets for her and asked if there was anything I could do. Our restaurant sent up crackers and water, and we tried to make her as comfortable as possible."

"As someone who has known life without a place to live," writes author Chris Horst, who interviewed Dave for *Christianity Today*, "he understands others wanting to call a place home, if even for a night."[1]

Dave also understands that satisfaction in his work is not ultimately found in status but in finding ways to serve the poor, the widow, the orphan, the foreigner, and—fittingly—the stranger who's far from home.

SACRIFICIAL SERVICE AND THE SAPP BROS. CHEYENNE TRAVEL CENTER

It's one thing to embrace customer service. It's quite another to live a life of sacrificial service.

Jesus calls his followers to "take up your cross and follow me." Peter wrote that serving as Christ did will entail suffering (1 Peter 2:21). It's easier to follow Christ when things are going well. But, in the words of biblical scholar Bruce Waltke, how many of us would qualify as the "righteous"—those willing to advantage others, even if it means disadvantaging ourselves?

People who commit to sacrificial service of a community through their work are rare. *New York Times* columnist David Brooks reported in his book *The Road to Character* that the median narcissism score has risen in the last two decades. When asked whether they agree with statements like "I am an extraordinary person," or "I like to look at my body," Brooks says, "ninety-three percent of young people score higher than the middle score just twenty years ago"— they score about 30 percent higher, to be exact.[2] Behind the thin veil of careers with social impact is often the Almighty Self, ever ready to find the perfect mix of social impact, comfortable work hours, and financial reward in "meaningful work." Especially since the pandemic, I believe the willingness to sacrifice for a cause greater than ourselves is diminishing.[3] Especially if it costs us.

Yet meaningful work is found not in success or financial reward but in sacrificial service. When people struggle to find a cause worth sacrificing for, boredom and meaninglessness tend to creep in. "Far too many people in this country seem to go about only half alive. All their existence is an effort to escape from what they are doing," wrote author and dramatist Dorothy Sayers about how most people view their work. "And the inevitable result of this is a boredom, a lack of purpose, a passivity which eats life away at the heart and a disillusionment which prompts men to ask what life is all about."[4]

People need a reason to sacrifice for something beyond themselves. It's what puts the wind in sails, feet on the ground, and energy in a workday. Paradoxically, what we're really looking for is the right cross to bear, not the best throne from which to rule.

We live in a cultural moment in which there are multiple issues calling for sacrificial work. Take, for example, the growing inequality in American society. In 1989, the Federal Reserve Reports that the bottom 50 percent held $22 billion in wealth while the top 10 percent held $1.7 trillion. Fast forward to 2021, and the bottom 50 percent held $260 billion in wealth while the top 10 percent swelled to $36 trillion.[5] To make that clearer, the top 1 percent of US households has fifteen times more wealth than the bottom 50 percent of households combined.[6] The simmering discontent and anger so prevalent in American society has a root, I believe, in millions of people seeing the wealthy get much wealthier—even in the last twenty years—while their standard of living stagnates or declines.

And yet, some decide that sacrificial love for others trumps personal comfort.

Julie (Sapp) Stone works as an investment director focused on family economic mobility at Gary Community Investments, a philanthropic organization. Before that she worked at Teach for America, an organization that places talented young teachers in low-income schools. Bright, energetic, connected, and committed, Julie was deeply formed by Catholic social teaching, which motivates her work on behalf of low-income families. When I asked Julie about her commitment to issues around justice, I was surprised to learn it came from growing up at a truck stop on the Wyoming-Nebraska border.

Julie's grandpa and his brothers were Depression-era survivors who bought a car dealership, which turned into car leasing and eventually into a small truck-stop chain headquartered in Omaha, Nebraska. Her dad became the general manager of Sapp Bros. Cheyenne Travel Center, and her mom the store manager. The establishment employed over a hundred people between a motel, gas station, restaurant, and store. Julie grew up just a few miles away and started to work in the family business alongside her brother at age five, picking up trash around the truck stop because of her parents' pride in their work. As she grew, she waited tables, stocked shelves, and served the truckers. Her dad would famously pause mid-bite while eating in the restaurant to check out a customer after their dinner because "nobody should have to wait to pay."

"I'll pound the table in defense of truck drivers. They are an extraordinary community," Julie says. "They're hardworking, responsible, God fearing, family centered, and make tremendous sacrifices for their work." Julie pauses, with almost reverence in her voice. "My dad always trusted that I'd be okay at the truck stop, whether he was there or not. Truckers know that their actions reflect on other drivers, which creates a sense of shared responsibility. If there was ever a conflict or a tactless comment, without fail, another driver would step in and sort things out."

Sapp Bros. was employee-owned, provided full health care coverage, and even paid for college tuition, which was practically unheard of in the 1980s. Julie's parents believed that their job was to lead and serve their employees sacrificially. "I remember one Christmas my dad had it out with corporate. Since the combined portfolio of travel stations didn't turn a profit that year, there would be no Christmas bonuses," she recalls. "I watched my mom and dad divide their past and future paychecks to make bonuses happen for the Cheyenne employees."

Julie believes her parents' leadership was built on love: "At the end of the day, Mom and Dad recognized that each employee was giving of their time and talent to help make our company successful. My parents were genuinely grateful for their people, which explains why so many who were hired on opening day in 1983 were still there when I graduated from college in 2003."

Julie's commitment to justice today isn't abstract. She sees the faces of those who worked for her parents for thirty years in frontline jobs—people of enormous integrity. "I see working families first. They show up for the physical work. They provide services and make products the rest of us rely on, they almost always go unnoticed. These are the families whose sacrifices benefit us all."[7]

SOULS AND SYSTEMS

A major challenge to engaging issues of justice for Bible-believing American Christians today is in our own theology. Salvation, it's often thought, is only a personal affair. I've sinned, Jesus pays for my sin on the cross, and now I'm saved and can enjoy a personal relationship with God in this life and the next. Salvation, it's often assumed, is primarily an experience for the isolated individual.

But this is only a fraction of the Christian story. "God was reconciling the world to himself in Christ," says the apostle Paul (2 Corinthians 5:19). Similarly, God was pleased to "reconcile to himself all things, whether things on earth or things in heaven, by making peace through his blood, shed on the cross" (Colossians 1:20). If sinful patterns can creep their ways into laws, traditions, and cultures, so can grace. Sin is both individual and systemic. So is redemption.

This reality of systemic sin has been common knowledge in Black communities for generations. Take, for example, the story of housing in American history. In 2016, the typical net worth of a White family was ten times greater (at $171,000) than the typical Black family ($17,150). That difference is due largely to discriminatory practices within the housing industry in the twentieth century. From 1934 to 1968, the Federal Housing Administration overtly discriminated against would-be Black homeowners, a practice known as "redlining." The FHA created color-coded maps indicating "risk levels" for long-term real estate investment, explicitly discriminating against Black communities by refusing to back loans to Black people or those who lived near them.

The long-standing policies had disastrous consequences for Black communities. Because home equity is generally the main way middle class people build wealth, denying access to loans created permanent disparities. In 2020, the national homeownership rate for Black families was 44 percent, while White families had a home-ownership rate of 73.7 percent. Even though redlining was outlawed over half a century ago, according to Redfin, the home-ownership rate for Black families has dropped in every neighborhood over the last forty years.[8]

If we believe, as we sing at Christmas, "He comes to make his blessings flow as far as the curse is found," we have to believe that redemption extends from individual experience to the policies, norms, and patterns of human behavior that make up so much of our shared lives. Emmanuel Katongole and Chris Rice write in their book *Reconciling All Things*,

> There is a widespread notion in some of the most energetic contemporary Christian movements that the biblical call to reconciliation is solely about reconciling God and humanity, with no reference to social realities. In this view, preaching, teaching, church life, and mission are only about a personal relationship between people and God. Christian energy is focused on winning converts, planting and growing churches, and evangelistic efforts.[9]

Yet, the "reconciliation of all things" would suggest that wherever there is the fracture of sin, Christ is at work healing those wounds through his people. Brian Gray of Denver Institute for Faith & Work writes that there are five places where God is at work in and through us in his work of redemption:

1. *Redemption with God.* Salvation is through God's atoning work on the cross, allowing for our union and communion with God.

2. *Redemption of our lives.* Sanctification includes our thoughts, words, and deeds, including our relationships, our feelings, our actions, and our motivations.

3. *Redemption with each other.* God is healing our relationships with each other through forgiveness and reconciliation.

4. *Redemption of systems and structures.* God's people are also called to address norms, practices, laws, traditions, and cultural assumptions in light of the biblical call to shalom, one part of which is right-relatedness in society.

5. *Redemption for the created world.* As stewards of the earth, we're called to care for God's world, which could include everything from environmentally friendly business practices to planting a tree with your family.[10]

Policies, company cultures, and even family traditions can make life harder or more dignified. They can be the glue that helps people work together in a common purpose at a distribution center or loading dock, or they can be the encrusted remnants of our fallen ancestors. The truth of the matter is that Christianity sees the need for the redemption of both individuals and institutions.

Martin Luther King Jr. famously said, "Injustice anywhere is a threat to justice everywhere. We are caught in an inescapable network of mutuality, tied in a single garment of destiny. Whatever affects one directly affects all indirectly."

Souls and systems are woven into a single thread of a cosmos yearning for redemption.

Professional Versus Working-Class Perspectives

Achievement Versus Struggle

Professionals see work as a chance to achieve and prove themselves. Many college-educated young adults, says David Brooks in *The Road to Character,* see work as the arena to maximize financial and psychological benefits while minimizing discomfort. Jobs are not about affording rent or childcare; they're how to make your impact on the world.

Many in the working class, however, see work as a constant struggle for survival. Job insecurity, dropping wages, and balancing childcare with work put constant stress on working-class families. As a result, many working-class families feel at a constant disadvantage.

Barbara Ehrenreich, author of *Nickel and Dimed: On (Not) Getting By in America*, decided to join the working class while writing her book by taking jobs as a waitress, nursing home aide, and Walmart salesclerk while living in motels and inexpensive trailer parks. She found that no job is truly "unskilled," that enormous mental and physical effort is needed to survive, and that often one job isn't enough—two are necessary if you want a roof over your head.

How does this feel? American rapper Eminem captures the working-class emotion in his Academy Award–winning song "Lose Yourself." He raps about having just one opportunity to seize what you wanted. And he does so waxing eloquent on living on food stamps, living in a trailer, and not letting failure be an option.

The feeling of being backed into a corner, needing to rise above circumstance, yet only having "one shot" illustrates the working-class dilemma. Life is not filled with many good choices; it's a constant struggle. Eminem is, I believe, wrong on lots of things. But he nails this experience perfectly.

For professionals, serving others sacrificially often means taking up the cause of the vulnerable with your cultural cachet. For the working class, it often means working hard, low-paying jobs or those with low prestige to provide for your family or community.

MAKING JUSTICE LOCAL

Huge cultural issues like hunger, access to clean water, corruption, or creating economic opportunity in areas of high poverty can seem overwhelming. But those who succeed in building a more just world start right where they are.

Savera Mutemariya has four kids and cares for eight more. She lives in Kigabiro, Rwanda, with her husband and for years depended on what they grew in their fields to support her family. "Getting food was hard, and I didn't have a house," remembers Savera. "I had three kids, but I wasn't even able to pay for primary school fees."

In 2006, Savera took out a small loan from a local bank to sell peanuts in a local market. "I started to realize, however, that I was capable." Eleven years later, Savera employs fifty people in her community and manages a supermarket, a hardware store, farming activity, a painting business, a carpentry and welding business, and several rental properties. As a result of her entrepreneurship, she has adopted eight orphans and helps employees pay for insurance and school fees. Savera says, "When you have a relationship with God, you understand that what God has given is for your benefit, but also for the benefit of those around you. I want to take what God has given me and use it to help people."[11]

Savera reminds me of three ideas from Christian theology that set a foundation for sacrificial service. The first is what Catholic theologians call subsidiarity, or the principle that social and political issues should be dealt with at the most immediate or local level. Rather than waiting for some CEO or elected leader to take care of our problems, each of us is responsible to solve the problems in our society. Pope Francis said, "The principle of subsidiarity allows everyone to assume their own role in the healing and destiny of society."[12] Savera did just that: she started with selling peanuts, and her work blossomed into an effort that served her entire community.

The second is the idea of Christian vocation, which simply means an entire life lived in response to the voice of God. Steve Garber, a writer and expert on the topic of vocation, believes that "vocation is integral—not incidental—to the mission of God."[13] Why? In a piece for *Comment* magazine, I wrote,

Vocation is a way to recover a sense of agency in a media-saturated world ruled by powerful tech, government, and media elites. In a culture of growing resentment, anger, and feelings of powerlessness over huge global issues—ranging from the war in Ukraine to a global pandemic—vocation says you can do *something*. It awakens individuals to their own ability to make a meaningful impact on their communities.[14]

Savera did just that; she responded to God's voice, she did *something*, and it turned into the healing of her community, a ripe example of God's mission in the world.

Third is a theology of place. Here I mean simply that God cares about the places where we live. He always interacts with us in particular times and places, and he calls us to take responsibility for the well-being of the places that we call home. John Stott wrote in his 1970s classic *Christian Mission in the Modern World*,

> If we are to love our neighbor as God made him, we must inevitably be concerned for his total welfare, the good of his soul, his body, and his community. When any community deteriorates, the blame should be attached where it belongs: not to the community which is going bad but to the church which is failing in its responsibility as salt to stop it from going bad.[15]

Each of us has a calling to care for our communities. This is what salt does: it flavors, but it also preserves what's good. And this too is what Savera did. She cared about her neighbors, and so she worked, she risked, and she loved.

VOLUNTEERING FOR JUSTICE OR WORKING FOR JUSTICE?

Many churches see the challenges of the world and often assume their primary role in addressing those issues is in organizing an "outreach" or calling members to volunteer at a local nonprofit. As good as volunteering is, members of the body of Christ are already touching nearly every major issue in the world today *through their occupations*. Christians gather together on Sunday, but during the week they are scattered into every corner of their cities as students, gardeners, financial advisers, bartenders, real estate agents, teachers, state representatives, coders, parents, soccer coaches, janitors, and executive assistants.

We don't simply serve God when we volunteer; we also serve when we meet the needs of others in our work. The question is whether we'll remain activated, integrated, and vibrant in our faith during the week, or whether we'll blend into the gray, dim, secular culture.

Christian history is filled with examples of men and women sacrificially serving others through their work. Florence Nightingale, for example, was an English social reformer, statistician, and the founder of modern nursing, which she pioneered when caring for wounded soldiers during the Crimean War. George Washington Carver was a botanist and agricultural innovator in the American South who called his lab at Tuskegee Institute "God's Little Workshop." Carver discovered that peanuts and soybeans could rejuvenate the soil and decrease dependence on cotton, which was the backbone of the slave economy. He believed God gave him these scientific discoveries, and, as it says on his tombstone, "He could have added fortune to fame, but caring for neither, he found happiness and honor in being helpful to the world."[16] Thomas Maclellan, whose Provident Insurance Company would produce nearly one billion dollars in total charitable donations generations after he was gone, simply prayed at the beginning of his career, "Use me, O Lord, I beseech Thee as an instrument for Thy service. May I bring some avenue of praise to Thee, and of benefit in which I dwell."[17]

Today, men and women of faith throughout the world are integrating sacrificial service of others into their daily work.

James Coleman, who started his career advocating for access to quality education, decided to run for public office to become a state senator out of conviction that God was calling him to better serve students, low-income workers, the formerly incarcerated, and economically vulnerable neighborhoods.

Allison Long Pettine, seeing that female founders raised just 2 percent of venture capital dollars in 2021, founded Ad Astra Ventures, helping women change the way they see themselves in business and helping them to fund, grow, and scale their businesses.

John and Ash Marsh committed to restoring their small town of Opelika, Alabama. They started by fixing up and selling just a few houses and eventually renovated hundreds of homes and started businesses ranging from restaurants to salons, all out of a commitment to "the resurrection of place."[18]

Each is motivated by their faith. Each reflects the image of the Suffering Servant of Isaiah 53 "who was pierced for our transgressions." Each faithfully does the small, good thing before them, bearing the "participation in his sufferings" for the sake of a far greater reward than this world can offer (Philippians 3:10; Hebrews 11:16).

And each decided their work could mean more than a paycheck. Through their jobs, despite all the pain and setbacks, they could taste the joy of God's kingdom in this world, in this time, and in this place.

A CUP OF COLD WATER

When Dave Collins goes to work each day as a housekeeper, he knows he can't do much about the fact that the average salary for a housekeeper in the United States is just $25,777, below the poverty line for those with families. He knows he can't solve the world's problems.

But he can answer calls with humility. He can smile at his co-workers. He can make a bed as if royalty were going to sleep there. And he can do his work remembering that even a cup of cold water given in the name of Jesus will one day be rewarded.

After a year of faithfully serving others in his job, Marriott awarded him for his service. At a fancy, downtown Denver banquet hall, he was given the Employee of the Year award for joyful service.

"I have a lot to do," Dave says. "I need to continue to show God's love to others. There are a lot of people who haven't yet seen it."

PART 3

Change

8

How to Change

My grace is sufficient for you, for my power is made perfect in weakness.

2 CORINTHIANS 12:9

It had been a hard week.

As I got out of the shower, my mind was spinning with the minor defeats of a middle-aged man. The time I lost my temper with my daughters at the dinner table. The day I felt about four inches tall when I was talked down to by somebody with more money and power than me. The crouching sloth I was silently battling when overwhelmed by too much to do and too little motivation. And then that Saturday afternoon on my back patio when I felt a wave of depression sweep over me.

That morning I looked at myself in the foggy mirror. Crow's feet had set in around my eyes. Gray hairs were sprouting from my sideburns. Alone in the bathroom, I said out loud, "God, when do I really change?"

I had been a Christian for twenty-two years, attended thousands of church services, and led a Christian organization, yet that day the promise of being conformed to the image of Christ had never felt so remote. Change, I've found the hard way, is elusive. Real, interior transformation—or what the New Testament simply calls abundant life—is the promise of the Christian gospel (John 10:10). And yet we struggle through addiction, broken relationships, and moral failures time and time again.

And it's not just a problem for Christian leaders blazing back to earth after a fall from grace. It's all of us. "Trying harder next time" seems to make it even worse.[1]

To become *good*—actually, thoroughly good—feels like grasping smoke on a windy day.

As I pass my fortieth birthday, one question sits behind every other question in my life: Who am I becoming? That is often followed by another: Can I really change?

HOW WE CHANGE

To be honest, I've become adept at finding new ways to say I'll change but then remaining stuck. The habits of sin—or even just the habits of our culture—have a way of reemerging like an unwanted trick birthday candle.

So, how do we change? Unfortunately, reading a book alone won't do it. This is sad news for an author. But I've come to believe that reading alone won't lead to real interior transformation. Think about your experience reading this book. Likely, it's before bed, after a hard day, or consumed in snippets on vacation or between sittings. Once you close the book—even if it's a self-help bestseller—you're still surrounded by anxieties, responsibilities, media, family, coworkers, and a thousand other noisy influences. It's not that books can't change you. I believe they can, but they rarely do so in isolation from the rest of life.[2]

How about getting more schooling? I'm a big believer in education, but many of our educational systems have largely adopted a narrow, heady version of change. Read a book, write a paper, take a quiz, then you'll change. And yet, in higher education or in high school, the curriculum that really changes people are the unwritten values and norms of a school—not just what the syllabus says.[3]

Most churches—at least word-centered Protestant churches— are similar. Though rarely stated, the unwritten message tends to be that the right combination of church attendance, music, and preaching will finally bring about the wholeness we desire. And yet, at least in my family, the van ride home from church often looks more like Chernobyl than the Garden of Eden. Some mysterious pattern of emotion, experience, and habit short-circuits even the most powerful experiences of God from creating real moral formation. I believe church is central to change, but we need to rethink what experiences actually lead to genuine Christian formation.

After researching the topic for years, I've discovered that trying to understand the way people change can leave you drowning in a quicksand of information: psychology, history, literature, sociology, andragogy, educational studies, history, theology, neuroscience, economics, current events, anthropology, sociology, philosophy—the author of Ecclesiastes wasn't wrong when he wrote, "Of making many books there is no end, and much study wearies the body" (Ecclesiastes 12:12).[4]

And yet, here we are, limping along. We're ever hoping things will get better, looking for salvation in every job offer, relationship, or vacation, yet feeling the subtle weight of encrusted sin, unhealthy habits, fractured relationships, and unmet dreams. If we really want to live a life that is truly healthy *from the inside out*, what kind of experiences might lead to real growth?

Unfortunately, I can't answer that question fully. I, too, am just learning. But I have a working theory I want to explore with you in this chapter:

Formation begins when an individual self-identifies *a problem, need, or point of suffering* and then joins a *high-commitment community*. The community is formed by an emotional and relational context of genuine vulnerability, bound together by a common *story or universal history*, and defined by a set of shared *habits and practices*.

Over time, change is solidified by a deeper engagement of *ideas and concepts* discussed in community that affirm the story; a *broader relational network* that exposes learners to new emotions, stories, ideas, habits, and practices; *significant work*, which the learner is called to perform using new skills and knowledge; and *public recognition* for accomplishment, which shapes the learner's identity.

Long-term change happens when the learner chooses to grow in *self-awareness* and cultivate new *spiritual disciplines*, which open the soul to the transformative power of the Holy Spirit.[5]

That's a mouthful. Let's take each of those movements one by one.

SUFFERING, COMMUNITY, AND VULNERABILITY

Squarely confronting suffering and pain is the beginning of change.

We all suffer. And our suffering is often the daily wounds that we tend to overlook, particularly in our families and work.

"If I hear another webinar that says, 'There's a lot of noise out there,' I'm going to lose it," says Lisa, a communications consultant. "I'm so tired. I just want to rest. Should I be looking for another job? Maybe I'm just adding to the noise."

A stay-at-home mom confesses, "I feel so alone. I thought I made the right decision to stay at home with the kids. But the mess, the schedule, the ingratitude . . . at least at work somebody appreciated what I did."

A nonprofit employee shares, "I can't give everything at work and then even more to my wife and kids at home. I'm empty. I have nothing more to give—I'm on the edge of addiction. I don't want it all to come crashing down."[6]

Life is filled with splinters—splinters we all experience. We try so hard to avoid suffering and pain, but it's when we turn *toward* our pain that we truly grow. John Ortberg, the former pastor of Menlo Park Presbyterian Church, says that when you ask people when they grew the most spiritually, 80 percent of the time they'll describe a difficult season—job loss, finances, or a stressed relationship.[7] Pain does not automatically create spiritual growth. Suffering can cripple and distort as much as it can strengthen. However, "suffering enables us to see the folly of chasing after temporal gods, and when people suffer, they often resolve to not return to their old way of life when things normalize." Suffering often leads to change because the status quo becomes more painful than the prospect of the unknown. "But you have a finite window of time to make changes," says Ortberg, "otherwise you drift back to old patterns."[8]

Most, however, miss this window of opportunity. The human instinct, says Jacques Philippe, a French Catholic monk and author of *Interior Freedom*, is to follow a pattern of rebellion or resignation rather than consenting to God using suffering to transform us. Our first reaction is to rebel against suffering by either coping or by trying to "fix" it. We reject reality and the hardships we face. We take either the route of seeking pleasure to forget our pain or do everything in our human power to fix the problem, assuming the role of God himself. When these strategies don't work, we often feel a sense of resignation or despondence. "This is just my lot. Things will never change," we say to ourselves. We wave a white flag.

Yet, change begins when we choose neither rebellion nor resignation but *consent* to God's presence inside of our suffering. "Consent leads to a completely different interior attitude," says Philippe. "We say yes to a reality we initially saw as negative, because we realize something positive may arise from it. This hints at hope."[9] The Christian recognizes that God is at work in all things, and can even turn evil into good, as he did at the cross. Consent is the interior willingness to stop running from pain and suffering, and let God shape us in the midst of suffering. As Pastor Tim Keller of Redeemer Presbyterian Church in New York City says, "Jesus didn't suffer on the cross so you would not suffer. He suffered so that when you suffer, you become more like Jesus."[10]

Once we decide to look squarely at our suffering rather than fleeing from it, the next step is to join a high-commitment community characterized by emotional and relational vulnerability.

Athletes on a high-performing team. Marines in basic training. Recently married parents with a newborn child. We often avoid commitments and want to "keep our options open" in a consumerist society. But we are most changed by the highest commitments we make, and then by opening our hearts to others in that community.

On March 14, 1948, Douglas Hyde handed in his resignation as the news editor of *The London Worker*. He had officially quit the Communist Party. He announced, instead, that he and his wife and children were joining the Catholic Church. Even though Hyde came to believe communism was antithetical to human flourishing, their methods, he believed, were extraordinarily effective in inspiring dedication. The party was able to incite people to make extraordinary sacrifices, make big demands on their members, and shape their hearts, minds, and vision for the world. "The Communists make far bigger demands upon their people than the average Christian organization would ever dare to make," Hyde writes. "They believe that if you make big demands on people, you will get a big response. . . . In the process, they have discovered that it is good psychology to ask for a lot. It is bad psychology and bad politics to ask for too little."[11]

This philosophy of change through high commitment sounds familiar. "Whoever wants to be my disciple must deny themselves and take up their cross daily and follow me" (Luke 9:23). It's no wonder that the early church did not just call people to belief but to join the church, a community of sacrificial commitment (Acts 2:42-47). The true benefits of church come not just with attending services but through membership. It's the church potluck, the small group, or the global mission trip that stir the pot of transformation more than just right doctrine.[12]

We also need to be willing to risk vulnerability. We must be up-front with our needs, our failures, and our shortcomings for communities to be truly transformative.

In my opinion, one of history's most transformative communities of emotional and relational vulnerability is Alcoholics Anonymous. The Twelve Steps begin with admitting "we are powerless over alcohol—that our lives had become unmanageable," and only "a Power greater than ourselves could restore us to sanity."[13] The legendary AA groups form a safe community of emotional and relational vulnerability where members can turn their lives over to God "as they understood Him," take an honest moral inventory, seek amends, and pray for help to change. Bill Wilson and Bob Smith, the founders of AA, now the world's largest and oldest alcohol recovery group, knew that change required facing our suffering, joining a community, and taking bold steps toward opening the heart to God and others.

NEW STORY, NEW HABITS, NEW PRACTICES

In the context of a high-commitment community, we then must re-evaluate the stories we've believed and the daily habits and practices that are shaping our character. The key questions for those wanting to change become: What stories define me and the world I live in? What habits are shaping me?

One of my former professors at Valparaiso University, Walter Wangerin Jr., was a master storyteller. I took a class from him on the Gospel of John as a junior, and I distinctly remember losing track of time in class, utterly transfixed by the stories he told. The African American congregation he served as a young pastor, the story of the Dun Cow (a children's book he wrote)—all found their way deep into my soul, almost as if bypassing the brain completely. "There have been religions without doctrines," he once declared in class, "but there have never been religions without stories."

Companies have stories (see chap. 9). Nations have stories. Films have stories. Families have stories. Each draws us in, as we feel that we too are in some kind of a story of our own, filled with drama, guides, decisions to make, and outcomes of both triumph and tragedy.[14]

The trouble comes when we've believed a false story about ourselves or the world. This could be a false philosophy or religion, but it could also be a false story we tell ourselves: "I need to control my kid's environment because if I don't, then I can't protect them from what I experienced." "My worth is found in my professional success. This is the only way I can face my former classmates." "The world is going to burn, anyway. I may as well give up and drown myself in pleasures."

The key to change is embracing what Lesslie Newbigin calls universal history. The Bible is, of course, a story, with beginnings, drama, climax, and resolution. But here's where it's different: it's both story *and history*, the single story of the way things are that reframes every other story. Here divine myth and human history become one. When we begin to reframe our political and economic theories—or our stories of family of origin—in light of salvation history, this is when change and healing take root.

And it does so when we simultaneously reevaluate the habits and practices that are shaping us. Much ink has been spilled on this topic, from James Clear's *Atomic Habits* to Charles Duhigg's *The Power of Habit*. A century ago, American historian and psychologist William James wrote, "Sow an action, you reap a habit. Sow a habit, you reap character; sow a character, you reap a destiny."[15] Millennia prior, Aristotle wrote in *Nicomachean Ethics* that "moral excellence comes about as a result of habit. . . . It makes no small difference, then, whether we form habits of one kind or another from our very youth; it makes a very great difference, or rather, *all* the difference."[16]

Habits really do change us, whether it's checking your smartphone ninety-six times a day[17] or going to church once a week. The monks knew this thousands of years ago (which is why spiritual disciplines, they believed, are not optional for those who want to change), and advertisers know it today. What we do habitually is who we become.

Change happens when, in the context of a high-commitment and vulnerable community, we start to lay out before others the foundational stories we believe and the habits that flow from those stories. This could be a small group at church, a group of friends, or a cadre of coworkers. Changing worldviews and habits by yourself is terribly hard. Doing it with others is the foundation of a changed life.

IDEAS, PEOPLE, WORK, AND FEEDBACK

Think of real change like you're building a house. The foundation is looking at your pain in a high-commitment community that is emotionally and relationally vulnerable. The rough framing, plumbing, electrical, and HVAC are the stories we believe and the habits and practices you do each day, week, and month. The drywall, trim, fixtures, and finishings are the ideas you know, the people you meet, the work you do, and the recognition you receive for that work.

First, ideas really do matter. I believe stories change us more than ideas, but ideas form the foundation of our beliefs. The "isms" of the twentieth century—fascism, communism, socialism, capitalism—caused world wars and shaped human history. Ideas we have about science or art, education or how to lay a concrete pad properly, all matter immensely. Those who want to solidify change in their lives start to get serious about the "renewal of their minds." They read, listen, and connect with others and ask them their views on what ideas are the most important to them. In 1936, John Maynard Keynes wrote, "The ideas of economists and political philosophers, both when they are right and when they are wrong, are more powerful than is commonly understood. Indeed, the world is ruled by little else."[18] If you want the walls of your interior castle to be plumb, you have to commit yourself to the pursuit of truth.

Second, your broader network or relationships shape you. Those outside of family and your "high-commitment community" set the horizon for what you believe is possible. For instance, Harvard researcher Raj Chetty found that the number one determinant in economic mobility is who you knew as a kid. Specifically, if low-income kids grew up around higher-income kids, they have a much higher chance of escaping poverty than if they grew up around other low-income kids.[19] If you want to change, you have to think about who your friends, and even your acquaintances, are (Proverbs 13:20).

Third, the work you do—and the feedback you get—also shapes you. D. Michael Lindsay, a college president and the author of books such as *View from the Top*, did a multiyear study on the White House Fellowship, a prestigious program for leadership and public service. He found that effective fellowship programs have four elements: a diverse cohort, a broad network, meaningful work, and public recognition. That is, programs that don't ask anything of participants don't influence them. You have to ask for something big. Also, public recognition tends to shape the learner's identity and signal to a community what they really value.

These both make sense to me. Taking risks in challenging work influences us. And what we praise also shapes us. When I praise my daughter for scoring a goal, it signals what our family values and in turn shapes her identity as an athlete. Conversely, researchers like Richard Reeves, a scholar at the Brookings Institution and author of *Of Boys and Men: Why the Modern Male Is Struggling, Why It Matters, and What to Do About It*, have found that when men lose a sense of pride and communal approval for their work, they wilt and communities suffer. When people clap for you—or when the clapping is noticeably absent—that too shapes you. For those wanting to change, it is worth simply asking the questions: What work am I doing, and how am I rewarded in that work? Is this making me more human, or something less than human?

The task here is to be intentional about what you learn, who you meet, the work you do, and how your identity is being formed by your work and your broader community.

SELF-AWARENESS, SPIRITUAL DISCIPLINES, AND GRACE

Your house of moral change is now built, but it's empty. For a house to be a home, it needs the warmth of laughter and the delight of people you love. The final step—and what I believe to be the long journey of real interior transformation that takes place over a lifetime—is the interplay between growing self-awareness and a deepening experience of God's grace through the practice of spiritual disciplines.

Interior freedom comes at the interplay of seeing ourselves as we truly are—that is, humility—and simply allowing God to transform us, accepting ourselves as God accepts us by his grace. We are free from needing to change ourselves or others because we trust that God himself is the final change agent. We can take stock of where we started and simply be honest about where we've grown and where we need to grow. We can live in peace, not because the world's issues are all solved but because we live our moment-to-moment existence *with* God, our friend. We do not become holy through effort; we become holy by association.

The byproduct of this deepening friendship is a deeper emotional resilience, deeper self-awareness, personal maturity, and personal humility. The fruit of the Spirit is experienced more frequently during times of prayer, confession, solitude, or worship—and even during times of setback, difficulty, or disappointment. Grace becomes the final reality.

Filmmaker Terrence Malick, in the opening monologue of his beautiful film *The Tree of Life*, captures the feeling of this kind of interior freedom. As scenes of a Midwestern family on a farm in the 1950s gently play out, we hear:

> The nuns taught us there are two ways through life, the way of nature and the way of grace. You have to choose which one you'll follow.
>
> Grace doesn't try to please itself. It accepts being slighted, forgotten, disliked. Accepts insults and injuries. Nature only wants to please itself. Get others to please it, too. Likes to lord it over them. To have its own way. It finds reasons to be unhappy when all the world is shining around it. And love is smiling through all things.
>
> They taught us that no one who ever loves the way of grace ever comes to a bad end.
>
> I will be true to you. Whatever comes.[20]

A TEN-YEAR JOURNEY AND CHANGE

Writing this chapter gave me pause. I believe that real change includes a combination of each of these three movements. I've seen it in others and in my own life. But where am I? As you can tell from this book, I still feel the storms inside. I believe change is possible, but have *I* really changed?

It was an emotional Tuesday afternoon. My wife, Kelly, and I walked into the Denver Institute for Faith & Work offices for the last time. Logo on the wall, new office, new furniture, and people that I've loved—and who've loved me—greeted us. It was a final chance for us all to share memories of ten years working together. I had let go; a talented new leader was ready to take the helm, and here we were, saying our goodbyes.

We sat, we ate, we reminisced, and we laughed. My coworkers shared memories of how my work had shaped them. A project, an event, a comment, a hard situation we got through together. As I looked at them as they intently shared their stories, I did so with near disbelief. Were these things really true about me? I could hardly push out of my mind all my shortcomings and failures during my leadership tenure.

But if I was honest, not only had God changed us together as a team over ten years; he had slowly changed me too. In community. Open and vulnerable, with new stories about work, practicing small spiritual disciplines over the years. Meeting new people, learning new ideas, working alongside others, and slowly, gently growing in awareness—and grace.

I'm certainly in progress, and my failures are daily. Yet I'm reminded of Paul's own experience of real change. "My grace is sufficient for you," he heard one day in a vision, "for my power is made perfect in weakness."

9

Translating
Your Convictions

To the Jews I become like a Jew, to win the Jews. . . . To those
not having the law I became like one not having the law . . . so
as to win those not having the law. To the weak I became weak,
I became weak, to win the weak. I have become all things to all
people so that by all possible means I might save some.

1 CORINTHIANS 9:20-22

In 2003, desperation filled the halls of Denver Public Schools.
Only 55 percent of Denver high school students graduated on time,
and that number dropped to 46 percent in 2008. But where most saw
hopelessness, Bill Kurtz saw opportunity. As a former banker with
JP Morgan Chase, Bill left New York City in 2003 to start a new
charter school. In 2004 Bill opened the Denver School of Science
and Technology (DSST) in Park Hill, one of Denver's most diverse
and underserved neighborhoods.

Despite the sparkling new science labs, the challenges of the
Denver Public School (DPS) system were daunting. DSST students
were 75 percent minorities and 45 percent from low-income households. But over the next decade, DSST would produce stunning

results. Average ACT scores rose to 24.6 (the DPS average is 17.6), 100 percent of seniors were accepted to a four-year college, and they had the fifth-lowest college remediation rate in Colorado.

"How have your schools been so successful?" I asked Bill over lunch at Udi's Bread Café in Central Park. In addition to clear goals and hiring well, Bill attributed success to "the culture we create," which is formed by their core values—respect, responsibility, doing your best, integrity, courage, and curiosity. He also uses language with his teachers and students of "the human story," noting "we all want to be affirmed for the gifts and talents we've been given."

In a context of public education, which is often antagonistic to outward displays of faith, Bill was careful to do the work of translating his convictions into a language his community could understand. A member of Denver Presbyterian Church, Bill says, "[Education] is a great place for me to live out my faith. Obviously, public education is a secular space, [but] there is an opportunity for me to live out my vocation, serving the needs of others and building strong communities."[1]

Though most see simply a charter school success story, there's another story his life tells. Bill's work in education is a symbol, a sign of a new world. New Testament scholar N. T. Wright believes Christians are called to "symbolic ways of doing things differently, planting flags in hostile soil, and setting up signposts that say there is a different way to be human."[2] Bill translated his faith into language his coworkers could understand and then took action. The result was a waterfall of hope for his entire community.

THE CHALLENGE OF TRANSLATING FAITH INTO A SECULAR WORKPLACE

"These ideas are fine," I've heard many people say, "but I work in a very secular company. How am I supposed to share my faith in a context where it's not invited—or is even condemned as inappropriate or offensive?"

It's a fair response to the ideas in this book. Home health care and software development, construction and biotech, driving trucks and driving profit margin are worlds far removed from church or faith-based nonprofits.

For most, the objection is twofold. First, the church has a language that isn't easily understood by the larger culture. Singing, Bible reading, sermons, and liturgies contain worlds like *sin, salvation, redemption, sanctification*, and *Eucharist*, words mostly unheard of in company policy manuals, Slack feeds, or break rooms. To make it worse, Christians often unthinkingly adopt insider language— "How's your heart, man?" "It was a total God thing," "Want to join my D group?"—that makes it even tougher to communicate faith to non-Christian coworkers or neighbors.[3]

Second, Christians often fear the consequences of speaking about their faith in the workplace. One investor I know, who held a prestigious job at a large asset management company, was quietly let go after sharing publicly about his faith at a Christian conference. His boss saw it as unprofessional and not in line with corporate culture. It's no different in, say, a hospital. Alyson Breisch, a scholar at Duke University who trains and teaches nurses, says that one of the concerns for faith-motivated nurses is that bringing up faith will cross professional boundaries, and that it may even be inappropriate in a physician-patient relationship.[4]

The task is to take up not just the vocation of one's work but also the vocation of *translation*. John Inazu, a legal scholar at Washington University in St. Louis and a Christian, knows this well: "My vocation of translation means translating the university to some of my church friends and translating the church to some of my university friends. Living between these two worlds makes me a kind of bilingual translator."

This work, he writes, often requires personal risk. One of Inazu's faculty colleagues said, "I don't get you; you're religious, but you care about poor people." On the other hand, those in his church have said they can't trust a "liberal law professor" like him.[5] Yet Inazu feels at home at the university and in church. And he's committed to helping to stand in the gap between two disparate worlds as an interpreter between church and his workplace. John believes we are "Christ's ambassadors, as though God were making his appeal through us" (2 Corinthians 5:20).

So how do we do it? How do people of faith translate their convictions about the biblical story into the secular workplace? Here's a place to start.

Discern what kind of environment you're in. Before you share the gospel at work, you must first understand the context in which you're working.

David Miller, who leads Princeton University's Faith at Work Initiative and is the author of *God at Work: The History and Promise of the Faith at Work Movement,* has proposed four postures companies usually take toward faith in the workplace.[6]

1. *Faith-avoiding.* In a faith-avoidant company, leadership has actively decided to avoid topics related to faith or religion. "That's not appropriate here," is the message, either explicitly or implicitly. On the more extreme side, religious employees fear being fired for expressing their beliefs, whether a Muslim wearing a headscarf or an evangelical Christian asking a coworker to accept Jesus as Lord.

2. *Faith-tolerant.* More common in companies, schools, hospitals, and government agencies is that faith is tolerated yet not embraced. Often, faith-tolerant organizations will provide religious accommodation to employees through the HR

department under the banner of diversity and inclusion. In larger companies, religious expression is often tolerated in "employee resource groups," yet it is rarely invited into the work or company culture itself.

3. *Faith-based.* The third option, which is most often cited among Christian networks of business leaders, is faith-based. In this model, the faith of company founders is woven into day-to-day operations of the company. This can mean the CEO is overt about his or her own faith in corporate communication, adopts religious symbolism in corporate culture, and groups, Bible studies, or evangelistic meetings take place at the workplace. This is common in smaller businesses or organizations led exclusively by Christians.

4. *Faith-friendly.* Miller advocates for a fourth option: faith-friendly. In a faith-friendly context, everybody's ultimate beliefs are welcome, whether those be Christian, Buddhist, or secular. In these organizations, leadership neither avoids or tolerates faith, yet neither do they assume employees share their convictions. Instead, it actively welcomes conversations about beliefs, backgrounds, and faith that shape employee's motivations.

In addition to Miller's four postures, I'd add the category *faith-persecuting.* In closed countries, such as Iran, or ideologically closed cities, like Boulder or Berkeley, being outward about your faith can have severe personal or professional consequences.

This four-part model can be helpful in understanding how faith can translate into your workplace. For instance, working in a dentist's office where all your coworkers are Christian will feel very different from working at a secular foundation that supports progressive causes. In one context you'll want to make space for others to speak who don't share your faith; in the other, you'll need to be covert about how your faith is expressed lest you become a pariah to your coworkers. Generally speaking, the larger the company you're in, the more it will slide toward the faith-tolerant or faith-avoiding side of the scale.

Should you find yourself in a context like this, you need to recognize that your company is not actually secular but a very "religious" place (Acts 17:22). Lesslie Newbigin believes, as do I, that companies not under the lordship of Christ are controlled not only by people but by what the New Testament calls "the powers and principalities." These powers, though created by Christ and for Christ, become corrupt and dark when they become absolute (Colossians 1:16; Ephesians 6). When Jesus disarmed the powers and principalities at the cross, he didn't destroy them but he did rob them of the claim to ultimate authority (Colossians 2:15). Though some see these verses as a hierarchy of demons and angels, language of power in the New Testament could also be applied to organizations, institutions, markets, or governments. This truth can help us see that when we go to work, various "gods" and ultimate purposes are already there, and we are ultimately in a missionary context.

Second, we need wisdom to be Christians inside broken systems. Again, Newbigin uses the language of subversion to understand the Christian's role in a company, industry, or system. For instance, when Paul deals with the runaway slave Onesimus, he does not call for an overthrow of the system of slavery but instead reorients Philemon's relationship to Onesimus in light of now being his brother in Christ. The gospel doesn't destroy systems but it sets them aright. "Undercover agents need a great deal of skill," Newbigin says. It's a real challenge to know what it means to be in consulting, psychiatry, or financial services as a Christian who recognizes that her industry or company is distorted by the fall.[7]

So, first, determine what kind of posture your workplace has toward faith and learn what the ultimate faith or worldview of your organization is. If it's in a place hostile the gospel or that's faith-avoidant, it will require discernment regarding how and when to share your faith. If it's faith-tolerant, you'll have to resist being "co-opted" into a pluralistic system. If it's faith-based, you'll need to make sure nonbelievers feel welcome and open to share their own beliefs. And if it's faith-friendly, you'll be able to take leadership in openly discussing faith in the workplace.

Reimagine your workplace culture in light of the gospel. The next step requires a work of the imagination. Ask yourself, What's good about my workplace or industry? What is distorted or fallen? What might it look like if it was healed? And what is God calling me to do about it right now?

These four questions mirror the four movements of the biblical story: creation, fall, redemption, and consummation. And they're worth asking regularly as you begin to consider what's good, broken, and possible about your company, school, firm, or clinic (see chap. 4).

For example, Trish Hopkins works as a real estate agent. "I'm astounded by whom God puts in my path. From a young sailor and his bride purchasing their first home to a World War II veteran selling his home after his wife's passing, daily I get to participate in history-making stories." Trish sees the goodness of her industry in helping people buy and sell homes, which is for many the largest and most significant purchase of their life. She also sees inflating home prices, stress-filled house hunting, and other agents who care little for their clients. She imagines a world where people would "build houses and dwell in them, they will plant vineyards and eat their fruit" (Isaiah 65:21). Her calling in this larger vision of "home" is simply to be a thoughtful, Spirit-filled relational presence, patiently helping home buyers and sellers navigate the process, and embrace an ethic of service, trust, and compassion.

In the book of Genesis, Joseph knew the power of Egypt and Pharaoh to unjustly imprison and persecute a religious and ethnic minority. But Joseph also believed that God could use Egypt for good, including saving thousands of lives by providing food during a famine (Genesis 50:20). He took a position of leadership in a corrupt government because he saw that God can, and does, use broken systems as a mysterious part of his redemptive plan.

Like Joseph, ask yourself, What role could even my broken, imperfect organization play in healing a small part of God's world?

Einstein once said, "Imagination is more important than knowledge." It is also central to seeing how faith may transfigure not just your own work but your whole industry.[8]

Decide what practices you'll engage in and which you need to abstain from. What are the distinctive activities or beliefs you want to champion at your organization as a Christian? And what are the practices or policies you must refuse as one ultimately committed to God's kingdom?[9]

For example, the prophet Daniel said yes to government leadership, serving in two different pagan empires. He believed his leadership as a Jew could be of service to God and witness to nonbelievers. He was willing to learn the language and literature of the Babylonians, and even take a foreign name. He also engaged in the regular practice of praying toward Jerusalem on company time. Yet Daniel and his fellow Jews Hananiah, Mishael, and Azariah also famously refused to follow the dietary practices of their peers, and they also refused to worship the CEO (Daniel 1–2). Ultimately, he was so valuable to his employer, Daniel's religious views were broadcast throughout the corporation (Daniel 3:29). This came through pursuing excellence in his work and carefully thinking through practices of engagement and abstention.

Sarah Eekhoff Zylstra, a journalist trained at Northwestern University, has covered everything from local politics for the *Daily Southtown* in Chicago to human interest stories for *Christianity Today*. Zylstra has seen journalism transform in the digital age and social media turn up the noise and heat around political and cultural issues. "The stories I write don't necessarily . . . have anything to do with the headlines of the day. We're looking for where God is at work," says Zylstra about what she chooses to write. She believes the gospel changes "how we see our sources." Because all people are image bearers, "we treat them very carefully. We want to have a lot of open communication with them. We come alongside them to tell their story, so my sources see my stories before they go up. It doesn't get sprung on them when the rest of the public sees." What she shares with her secular peers is a commitment to getting accurate information and double-checking facts. Yet in contrast to the never-ending anxiety-driven news cycle, her journalism is countercultural in its focus on local stories, where people tend to be more hopeful about their communities and lives.[10]

Deciding what practices to engage in and which to abstain from requires discernment. You may see your coworkers in a tech company disengaging from their work and embracing an "age of anti-ambition," as one *New York Times Magazine* writer put it. Yet your response might be to embrace a deep practice of sabbath rather than slack off in your work. Your school may have strict, unspoken rules about sharing your faith with coworkers, but you might instead choose to embrace intentionality with nonbelievers as a spiritual discipline. Your financial services firm may be driven by greed or fear of missing out on maximal returns, but you might instead practice contentment, or simply letting your yes be yes or your no be no, resisting the temptation to twist language to close deals for maximal personal benefit (Matthew 5:37).

To be a Christian in a secular age requires a form of civil disobedience, a refusal to comply with the patterns of this world (Romans 12:2). It also requires Christians to offer alternatives, finding practices that "give an answer to everyone who asks you to give the reason for the hope you have. But do this with gentleness and respect" (1 Peter 3:15).

Embrace the power of language. "What's our motto? Practically, it's profit, profit, and more profit." Scott shares his story with me over breakfast at GraceFull Cafe in Littleton, Colorado. He works at a large private equity firm, a company that buys and sells other businesses.

As Scott finishes a breakfast burrito, his expression changes, and his countenance becomes lighter. "But here's what I do. On my whiteboard in my office, I write my values which guide how I work and serve in business: integrity, humility, excellence, grace, and joy. I start conversations about them with employees, CEOs I mentor, even partners at the firm." For Scott, the language he uses about his work is a bridge to conversations about faith.

Most of us aren't CEOs who can just rewrite a company's values. But we can intentionally choose which values we can get behind, and then we can carefully "lead up" and challenge the company to live up to its own best version of itself. Language can be a powerful way to do this.

For example, David Bailey leads a nonprofit in Richmond, Virginia, called Arrabon, which focuses on racial reconciliation. Rather than using language of diversity, equity, and inclusion, which has become a source of tension in many communities, he speaks of God calling us to form reconciling communities that lead to "proximity, empathy, and then unity." He believes that the work of racial justice must first have a foundation in spiritual formation.

Another exemplary leader using language to build value-oriented work is a friend I'll call Steve, who started a fintech company in the mortgage industry. He counsels other business owners to look at the overlap between your "cultural why," your "company why," and your "kingdom why."

Steve saw that the net worth of a typical White family was nearly ten times greater than that of a Black family, and that home ownership was *the* difference between this huge asset differential. Steve saw a cultural need, and his "kingdom why" was based on a desire to see shalom and justice in his community. So he created a company that helps small- and medium-size lenders efficiently process mortgages, offering both a competitive advantage for local lenders as well as designing a product that can ultimately help get more people, including people of color, into homes. The intersection of his three "whys" formed a company built on the values of rigor, ownership, curiosity, kindness, and transparency.

Distinctive language in a secular culture focuses on the individual. Self-esteem, personal empowerment, and various shades of self-aggrandizement dominate. Yet Christian language is uniquely grounded in grace. Words like faith, hope, and love—the three theological virtues—draw listeners into a gospel-centered world. Language of thriving, human flourishing, or the common good can become common ground that draws coworkers into deeper conversation about the very purpose of work.

I personally tried this exercise. I wanted to see if I could translate our principles—think theologically, seek deep spiritual health, create good work, embrace relationships, and serve others sacrificially—for a broader audience. I wrote an article titled "Designing Workplaces to Be More Human" and encouraged readers to ask these questions that could be transferred to any secular context:

- Do we invest in deep emotional and spiritual health?
- Do we encourage real friendship and relational wholeness?

- Do we create conditions for people to do their best work?
- Do we stimulate broad thinking about the key issues of our day?
- Do we really care about our city, especially the vulnerable?[11]

Language is powerful. Think about the words you'll repeat, the words you write, and the words you speak as ways to create bridges into the biblical story.

Tell more beautiful stories. My four daughters and I like to read before bed. We've maintained the tradition from when they were toddlers to their teenage years. One of our favorite passages is in C. S. Lewis's *The Silver Chair.* In the scene, Jill Pole is incredibly thirsty and in search of water. She arrives at a flowing stream and she becomes ten times thirstier when she sees it. But she pauses: a lion is lying down next to the stream.

She faces a conundrum—if she goes to the stream, she may be eaten by the lion. If she runs away, she might perish from thirst. But all she can focus on is the water because of her thirst. The lion says, "If you're thirsty, you may drink." She feels a tinge of fear and freezes. The lion says again, "Are you not thirsty?" Jill replies, "I'm dying of thirst." "Then drink," the Lion says.

Jill says, "Would you mind going away while I do?" The lion gives her a look, and a low growl. Now the rippling of the stream is driving her almost crazy with thirst. Jill responds, "Will you promise not to do anything to me, if I do come?" The lion says, "I make no promise." Jill, forlorn, says, "I daren't come and drink."

The lion replies, "Then you will die of thirst."

Crestfallen, Jill says, "I suppose I must go and look for another stream then." But the lion simply says, *"There is no other stream."*

Stories can speak the truth more clearly than statements. In the modern workplace, people will likely look at you strangely if you tell them "Jesus is the only God and the only way to be saved." But you might get a smile if you tell a story about a small girl and a lion.

Though we're often afraid to share the gospel with our coworkers, the truth is that our culture is constantly consuming stories. The reason Apple, Amazon, Netflix, and Disney are waging the streaming wars is because people are searching desperately for meaning, for a story they can eat and satisfy their soul. Jesus knew this, which is why parables were the main medium he used to communicate the gospel of the kingdom.

This too requires tact. Emily Dickinson counsels us to "tell all the truth but tell it slant," so that people will experience "superb surprise." "The Truth must dazzle gradually" or people cannot behold the light.[12] Those who tell the best stories have the power to shape culture, a truth that civilizations and cultures have known for centuries.

Your place of work is a great place to tell gospel-oriented stories. The distinctive aspect of a Christian story is *love of others through self-sacrifice*. Along with distinctive practices, highlighting, for instance, the way a soldier died for his fellow Marine or a lawyer who took the blame for the mistakes of a junior coworker has the power to redeem an entire organizational culture.

AMBASSADORS FOR CHRIST

A charter school leader. A nonprofit employee. An asset manager. A tech founder. A journalist. Translating the gospel in your industry is not without peril, but it is possible.

And when God's people do this hard work, they join a great company of saints who represent the living God to their generation (Hebrews 11). And they join the apostle Paul, who, having seen the resurrected Christ, said "I have become all things to all people so that by all possible means I might save some" (1 Corinthians 9:22).

10

A Life of Love

*A new command I give you: Love one another. As I have loved
you so you must love one another. By this everyone will know
you are my disciples, if you love one another.*

JOHN 13:34-35

As it turns out, Christians throughout history have always
been innovators.

If you had lived hundreds of years ago in the shame-honor culture
of pagan Europe—the Anglo-Saxons, the Franks, the Germans—
you would have thought the ethic of forgiving your enemies and
caring for the poor and weak to be a ludicrous, unworkable concept.
The idea that even the most vulnerable have value—because they're
made in God's image and Jesus died for them on the cross—was a
Christian innovation.

Say you lived in ancient Greece, the birthplace of democracy. Giving
slaves and women the right to vote would likely have never crossed your
mind. That innovation, too, came from the Christians. Scholars like
Brian Tierney of Cornell University showed that universal human rights
and the equality of every individual didn't come from secular philosophers in the seventeenth and eighteenth centuries but instead from
twelfth-century Christian canon lawyers. And it was Christian scholars

whose ideas led to limiting the power of kings, and ultimately to the Magna Carta, which many see as the root of our republican system of government today. Universal human rights? Again, innovators.[1]

How about women's rights, including the idea that sex between a man and a woman should always be consensual? Or the idea that you should be benevolent to all people, not only your tribe? You guessed it: the Christians.[2]

Other scholars, like historian Tom Holland, have shown that modern science was born in traditionally Christian countries, and not in the Far East countries dominated by Hinduism or Buddhism. Christians believed the world was real, not an illusion, and that the Creator governed it by discoverable and regular laws, not through arbitrary decisions, like the gods of ancient Greek myths. Modern science, again, was an innovation that took root first in Christian lands.[3]

Yet the strangest innovation of all may have been the idea of love.

Today we see "love" written on T-shirts and kitchen wall hangings, and we hear in popular songs, "All you need is love." But if you lived in, say, ancient Rome, all spoils went to the powerful, and the all-out pursuit of power was heralded as *the* way to organize a society. It was dominance, not love of neighbor and care for the overlooked, that ruled the world. Through the ages Christians recentered the world on the idea of a God who is at his core self-giving love.[4]

Indeed, sacrificial love is *the* defining mark of the Christian.[5]

FROM THE INSIDE OUT

We started this book with a sober look at reality: the number of church members in the United States is its lowest in modern history, the number of self-professed Christians is plummeting, and we are deeply divided and fragmented. Poet William Butler Yeats wrote, "The falcon cannot hear the falconer; / Things fall apart; the center cannot hold." In a time when "falcons" are losing the voice of their Caller, can society hold together?

I believe it can. But it requires not just a new program, campaign, or initiative. It requires first that Christians, the salt and light of culture, first become a certain kind of people. The great challenge for the body of Christ today is not to transform society but to transform ourselves. The question we should be asking is not how we change the world. It is first, who are we becoming?

If we are going to become people of love who can clearly reflect the love of their Creator to an unbelieving world, it will require transformation from the inside out.

I've argued in this book that transformation takes place first in our interior world, then in our exterior life, and finally in our civic life.

It begins by *seeking deep spiritual health* and embracing the conviction that deep inner transformation of our emotions and our souls is core to living a fully human life. It includes *thinking theologically*, a pursuit of truth and wisdom centered on God's revelation. Change begins in our interior worlds.

Second, transformation occurs when we *embrace relationships* and *create good work*. As we allow the Spirit to work within, faith takes on exterior expressions through our daily interactions with family, coworkers, and neighbors, and through our Christian vocations. Change moves to the exterior world.

Finally, change influences our communities when we take on the challenge of leadership and *serve others sacrificially*, humbly caring for the vulnerable and doing our part to address the big social, economic, and cultural issues of our day. Change finally moves into our civic life.

The final result: a single, holistic life of love, received and understood, expressed and embodied, and finally systematized in our organizations, businesses, cities, and cultures.

Transformation from the inside out is what our world needs. And this is what each of us longs for.

THE WHOLE STORY

These five principles are a way forward for all of us working to integrate faith and work. And the order of transformation matters, as well as the inclusion of all five of these principles.

Transformation "from the outside in" is the standard operating procedure for a secular culture. The hope is that if we create just the right policy, have the right social program, or make a big enough impact with our work, then not only will the world be made right, so will we. Unfortunately, this simply isn't true for a simple, solitary reason: sin. Something is at the root inside of us that we cannot dislodge by ourselves, and if we ignore it, all our programs for social, cultural, or economic triumph will turn to dust. Transformation from the outside in, without inner restoration, is more like disfiguration.

It also matters that we have all five principles. What if, say, we were to remove one of the five principles, such as *create good work*? How would it influence our vision for a life of faith?

SEEK DEEP
SPIRITUAL HEALTH

EMBRACE
RELATIONSHIPS

THINK
THEOLOGICALLY

SERVE OTHERS
SACRIFICIALLY

Discipleship without our daily work can be theologically thoughtful, kind toward others, and potentially engaged with the social issues of our day. But it misses the majority of our waking lives. And it misses the obvious truth that work is where we have the chance to individually make a public contribution. Work is central to human life, as well as the Christian life.

What if we removed *seek deep spiritual health* and *embrace relationships* from the equation?

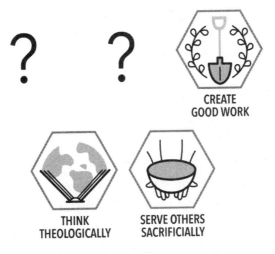

CREATE
GOOD WORK

THINK
THEOLOGICALLY

SERVE OTHERS
SACRIFICIALLY

If we have theology, work, and cultural engagement but lack spiritual formation and relational health, we have a version of Christianity that's smart but spiritually thin. We may have the right answers and get involved in big social campaigns, but what good is gaining the whole world if we lose our very own souls? This is a version of faith that tends to be about power rather than love, "changing the world for Christ" rather than allowing Christ to first change us. Without spiritual and emotional health, we may become "successful," but we'll never be whole.

What if we tossed out *think theologically?* What would that mean for our faith?

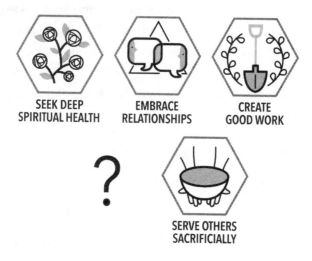

Without learning and understanding the biblical story, the historic doctrines of the faith, and their relevance for our world today, we have no framework for understanding ourselves, the human condition, our world or our work. Those who relegate doctrine as "just for academics" are also those who, as James says, are like a "wave of the sea, blown and tossed by the wind" (James 1:6). Theology is a strong foundation on which we can stand in a tumultuous culture. This version of Christianity might be nice, but it's not transformative.

One last question: What if we were to remove *serve others sacrificially* and the biblical traditions of justice and cultural engagement from our practice of Christianity?

This version of faith and work devolves into "me, Jesus, and my job," forgetting both the consistent themes in Scripture of concern for the vulnerable and responsibility for the well-being of our communities as an expression of neighborly love. But more importantly,

it misses the joy of shalom, a life of sacrificial love poured out for others. The upside-down kingdom of the Messiah is shown when we recognize that, in the well-known words of Martin Luther King Jr., "the arc of the moral universe is long, but it bends toward justice."

To live out the gospel in our lives, we need all five—even those principles we're not especially drawn to. If God's love lives in us, he will live in our hearts, our minds, our relationships, our work, and our society.

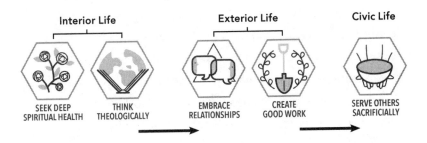

RESERVOIRS, NOT CANALS

So often our lives are not as we long for them to be. Rather than the fruit of the Spirit, our emotional lives are anxious, depressed, and empty. Rather than a life guided by truth, we depend on slogans, social media, and half-truths. Rather than healthy relationships in our families and workplaces, we settle for fractures and wounds. Rather than work filled with purpose, we do what we must to get through the day. Rather than justice and restoration, we swim in a sea of resentment, anger, and societal division.

But it doesn't have to be that way.

Healing *is* possible. We can choose to allow our convictions and our actions, our words and deeds, to flow from the same source of life.

The longer I've sat with this book, and asked questions about my own life, the more I've returned to the question: Who am I becoming? What is really inside of me, and what kind of "fruit" do I really grow? Am I drawn more to the four great temptations throughout human history—wealth, power, pleasure, and fame—or the theological virtues of faith, hope, and love?[6] And when I see outbursts of anger come from within, what am I to do?

The key is to first allow God to fill our souls with his living water. Bernard of Clairvaux, a twelfth-century Cistercian abbot, once wrote, "The man who is wise, therefore, will see his life as more like a reservoir than a canal. The canal simultaneously pours out what it receives. The reservoir retains the water till it is filled, then discharges the overflow without loss to itself." For years, I had lived more like a canal, eager and ready to "take the next hill," work to the bone, and press my capacity to the edge. Yet the canal would often run dry. Depleted, my spirit sagged, my resilience wore thin, and those around me paid the price.

The image of a reservoir, filled with the immensity of God's mercy and grace, however, was a completely new thought. Could I have so much of God's living water that the challenges I face each day wouldn't deplete the well of life within? As the prophet Isaiah proclaims,

Come, all you who are thirsty,
    come to the waters;
and you who have no money,
    come, buy, and eat!
Come, buy wine and milk
    without money and without cost. . . .
Listen, listen to me, and eat what is good,
    and you will delight in the richest of fare. (Isaiah 55:1-2)

God is offering to us, free of charge, what we all truly long for.

The invitation of this book is not to begin with external markers of success. It is to first receive. To first wait on God's life and healing before we heal others. "You too must learn to await this fullness before pouring out your gifts," says Bernard. "Do not try to be more generous than God."[7]

Do not live from the outside in. Live from the inside out. Choose to become a reservoir, overflowing with life *from* God *for* the world.

A LIFE OF LOVE

In a fragmented culture that is quickly losing faith, how will the church regain its winsome public witness? What would a broad movement of men and women taking this interior-to-exterior-to-civic journey accomplish?

I believe it would spur a growth of Christian belief, as theology moves from the private spheres of church and family to the public spheres of work across industries. People would sow the seeds of emotional and spiritual health in their families, workplaces, and communities. Healthy, humble relationships would multiply through broad professional networks, healthy friendships, and a love of our cities. The healing of work would result in healthy motives for our jobs, coherence between our faith and our work, and growing Christian leadership across sectors. And each Christian would embrace biblical justice, committing to serving the vulnerable in our places of influence and addressing the most pressing issues we face today with the skills, talents, and opportunities in our everyday lives.

And this would happen principally through our everyday lives, in our families and through our work. Os Guinness prophetically wrote,

> Grand Christian movements will rise and fall. Grand campaigns will be mounted and grand coalitions assembled. But all together such coordinated efforts will never match the influence of untold numbers of followers of Christ living out their callings faithfully across the vastness and complexity of modern society.[8]

We need not wait for others to take action. God is summoning *us*, right here and right now.

Externally, society would see Christians—and Christianity—in a new light, fulfilling Christ's words, "By this all people will know that you are my disciples, if you love one another." Internally, the fragmentation that found its way into our souls would subside, as Jesus promised rest:

> Are you tired? Worn out? Burned out on religion? Come to me. Get away with me and you'll recover your life. I'll show you how to take a real rest. Walk with me and work with me—watch how I do it. Learn the unforced rhythms of grace. I won't lay anything heavy or ill-fitting on you. Keep company with me and you'll learn to live freely and lightly. (Matthew 11:28-30 MSG)

It begins with us—each of us—being willing to take the journey of transformation from the inside out.

HEALING OUR WORK, OUR WORLD

"The highest reward for a person's toil," said John Ruskin, the nineteenth-century English writer, "is not what they get for it, but what they become by it."[9]

Rather than work being a place of necessary but dreaded toil or the self-focused medium to make our imprint on the world, work can shape us. God is already initiating, inviting us into his triune life, and working inside us. He is summoning us to work alongside him, and in so doing, become like him.

The task before us is simply to take the next step toward change. To turn toward our suffering, join a community, be vulnerable, and reassess our stories, our habits, and our deepest held beliefs. A small step of courage can shape a life.

Over time I learned more about Brent, the liquor distribution manager. Years ago, one of his parents died and it left an interior scar he struggled to cope with. Anxiety and feelings of despair became a constant struggle. "But that's not the final word on me," Brent told me recently, reflecting on the journey. "I'm going to church. I'm meeting with a counselor. And I'm trying to make friends with other guys."

Brent said he's reconsidering how he works and why he works. He's applying for a new job within his company. "I don't really get into that CEO stuff," he says, referencing his friends who've "done better than me." But "I do think God can heal what's going on inside of me. And if he can heal me, he could heal anyone."

Brent gives me hope. He reminds me that we're all in process. And we do have a choice.

Each of us can take the next step in learning to live and work from the inside out.

Acknowledgments

When I take my seat in an airplane, I usually tune out the safety protocols. However, I do pay attention when the flight attendants give instructions about those yellow oxygen masks. First, they say, put the mask on yourself. Only then should you attempt to put it on somebody else. It's good advice.

Writing a book about Christian formation and work is a humbling experience. With each chapter, I recognize both my own shortcomings, and the friends, family, and coworkers who have shown me what it means to put on that yellow mask and breathe in new life.

First, let me thank you, the reader. There would be no books without readers. Your attention is the most valuable asset you have, and you have my sincere gratitude for loaning it to me. Also, let me ask for your grace. I intended to write this book for any worker, and yet because of the limitations of my own knowledge and my own work experience, I mentioned professional voices far more than working-class ones. My next book, *God of the Second Shift*, will further address issues central to blue-collar and pink-collar workers. If you're a working-class man or woman, I'd be deeply grateful to hear the story of your work as I'm working on my next book. Please reach out to me at www.jeffhaanen.com/contact.

Second, this book is drawn from years of people, experiences, and ideas through my work at Denver Institute for Faith & Work. For all who've come to an event, been fellows, downloaded a podcast, led a similar initiative in other cities, or shared your stories with me, thank you. I want to give a special thank you to my coworkers and colleagues who've so shaped my own journey from 2012 to 2022. I'd like to personally thank Brian Gray, Doug Smith, Jill Anschutz, Joanna Meyer, Jeff Hoffmeyer, Ross Chapman, Abby Worland, Lisa Slayton, Bob Larkin, Catherine Sandgren, Pamela Ramon, Hunter Beaumont, Chris Horst, Jim Howey, Drew Yancey, Cindy Chang Mahlberg, Cliff Johnson, Dustin Moody, Ryan Tafilowski, Bob Cutillo, Olivia Duncan, Jeanne Oh Kim, Eric Most, Adam Hasemeyer, Matt Turner, Darius Wise, Chuck Stein, and Marcy McGovern.

I also want to thank my editors, Liz George, Jessica Schroder, Al Hsu, and the team at InterVarsity Press. Books really are quite a jumbled mess (at least mine are) without the careful, refining hand of a good editor. You have my gratitude. And a special thank you to my dear friend and literary agent Andrew Wolgemuth. You opened a door for me I could not have opened for myself.

I want to thank my daughters, Sierra, Lily, Alice, and Cora. They extended kindness, love, and patience as I wrote this book. (Lily, in particular, brought me a chocolate chip cookie while grinding through a last round of revisions.) It's because of them more than anyone else that I've asked the question, who am I becoming?

Finally, I want to thank Kelly, my wife. You, more than anyone, have extended grace to me as I've attempted to take the journey from the inside out. In the midst of my storm, your example and friendship continually whisper to me, "Peace."

You are a gift.

Notes

1. FRAGMENTED LIVES, FRACTURED CULTURE

[1] Gallup, "Workplace Employee Engagement Holds Steady in First Half of 2021," www.gallup.com/workplace/352949/employee-engagement-holds-steady-first -half-2021.aspx.

[2] "PwC US Pulse Survey: Next in Work," www.pwc.com/us/en/library/pulse -survey/future-of-work.html.

[3] Heather Long, "It's Not a Labor Shortage, It's a Great Reassessment of Work in America," *Washington Post,* May 7, 2021, www.washingtonpost.com/business /2021/05/07/jobs-report-labor-shortage-analysis/.

[4] Kim Parker and Juliana Menasce Horowitz, "Majority of Workers Who Quit a Job in 2021 Cite Low Pay, No Opportunities for Advancement, Feeling Disrespected," *Pew Research Center,* March 9, 2022, www.pewresearch.org/fact -tank/2022/03/09/majority-of-workers-who-quit-a-job-in-2021-cite-low-pay -no-opportunities-for-advancement-feeling-disrespected/.

[5] Gene Marks, "Turns Out the Great Resignation May Be Followed by the Great Regret," *The Guardian*, March 20, 2022, www.theguardian.com/business/2022 /mar/20/great-resignation-great-regret-employees-quitting.

[6] Robert Putnam, *Our Kids: The American Dream in Crisis* (New York: Simon & Schuster, 2016). See also Anne Case and Angus Deaton, *Deaths of Despair and the Future of Capitalism* (Princeton, NJ: Princeton University Press, 2020).

[7] Derek Thompson, "Workism Is Making Americans Miserable," the *Atlantic,* February 24, 2019, www.theatlantic.com/ideas/archive/2019/02/religion -workism-making-americans-miserable/583441/.

[8] Nicholas Eberstadt, "Education and Men Without Work," *National Affairs,* Winter 2020, www.nationalaffairs.com/publications/detail/education-and -men-without-work.

[9] Arthur Brooks, "The Dignity Deficit," *Foreign Affairs*, March/April 2017, www.foreignaffairs.com/articles/united-states/2017-02-13/dignity-deficit.

[10] "Loneliness in America: How the Pandemic Has Deepened an Epidemic of Loneliness and What We Can Do About It," Harvard Graduate School of Education, February 2021, https://mcc.gse.harvard.edu/reports/loneliness-in-america.

[11] Vivek H. Murthy, "Protecting Youth Mental Health," US Surgeon General's Advisory, 2021, www.hhs.gov/sites/default/files/surgeon-general-youth-mental -health-advisory.pdf.

¹² "Generation Z and Mental Health," Annie E. Casey Foundation, October 16, 2021, www.aecf.org/blog/generation-z-and-mental-health.

¹³ Pew Research Center, "In US Decline of Christianity Continues at Rapid Pace," October 16, 2019, www.pewforum.org/2019/10/17/in-u-s-decline-of-christianity-continues-at-rapid-pace/.

¹⁴ While I don't believe American or Western culture has fully realized a golden age, or one in which life was completely whole and integrated, many have made the argument that Christian influence, minimally, is waning, and by many measures, life since the 1960s has indeed gotten worse for many low- and middle-income Americans. See Ross Douthat, *Bad Religion* (New York: Free Press, 2013); and Robert Putnam, *The Upswing* (New York: Simon & Schuster, 2021).

¹⁵ See Joan C. Williams, *White Working Class: Overcoming Class Cluelessness in America* (Boston: Harvard Business Review Press, 2017). Also, for the contrasts between professional and working-class perspectives, see Jeff Haanen, "Six Differences Between How Professionals and the Working-Class See Their Daily Work," October 12, 2018, http://jeffhaanen.com/2018/10/12/six-differences-between-how-professionals-and-the-working-class-see-their-daily-work/.

¹⁶ Jeff Haanen, "God of the Second Shift," *Christianity Today* 62, no. 8 (October 28, 2018): 34-41.

2. FROM THE INSIDE OUT

¹ Don Flow, "Driving Trust," Center for Faithful Business, Seattle Pacific University, YouTube video, 6:52, www.youtube.com/watch?v=IEDwJialwZg.

² Lesslie Newbigin, *Foolishness to the Greeks: The Gospel and Western Culture* (Grand Rapids, MI: Eerdmans, 1988).

³ "David Foster Wallace on Life and Work," reprint of his 2005 commencement address at Kenyon College in 2005, *Wall Street Journal,* September 19, 2008, www.wsj.com/articles/SB122178211966454607.

⁴ The 5280 Fellowship is a nine-month program for emerging leaders in Denver focused on spiritual formation, professional development, and civic engagement. Brian Gray, the 5280 Fellowship Director, describes the core goal of the program as a life lived "with God, for the world, through our work." For more information, visit 5280fellows.com or citygate.com.

⁵ These five principles and icons are from Denver Institute for Faith & Work. See www.denverinstitute.org/guiding-principles.

⁶ C. S. Lewis, *The Weight of Glory* (New York: HarperOne, 2001), 116.

⁷ "Jennifer Wiseman Makes Sure Hubble Brings the Night Sky to Us," NASA, October 29, 2019, www.nasa.gov/feature/goddard/2019/jennifer-wiseman-makes-sure-hubble-brings-the-night-sky-to-us.

[8] Dave Meyer's story is taken from an onstage interview at Vocational Stewardship for the Common Good: https://denverinstitute.org/event/vocational-steward ship-common-good/.

[9] For more, see Jeff Haanen, "Six Differences Between How Professionals and the Working Class See Their Daily Work," October 12, 2018, https://jeffhaanen .com/2018/10/12/six-differences-between-how-professionals-and-the-working -class-see-their-daily-work/.

[10] "Christians in the Public Square," *The Faith & Work Podcast*, Denver Institute for Faith & Work, https://denverinstitute.org/s3e7-christians-public-square/.

[11] For a humbling overview of growing wealth inequality in America in the last fifty years, see "Nine Charts about Wealth Inequality in America," https://apps .urban.org/features/wealth-inequality-charts/.

[12] This story first appeared in Jeff Haanen, "Light for Electricians: How Christians Bring Hope to Business," *Christianity Today*, March 21, 2016, www.christianity today.com/ct/2016/march-web-only/light-for-electricians-christians-bring -hope-to-business.html.

[13] Dallas Willard, *The Great Omission: Reclaiming Jesus's Essential Teachings on Discipleship* (New York: HarperOne, 2014).

3. SEEK DEEP SPIRITUAL HEALTH

[1] Curt Thompson, *The Soul of Shame: Retelling the Stories We Believe About Ourselves* (Downers Grove, IL: InterVarsity Press, 2015).

[2] "Whole-Hearted Leadership," Denver Institute for Faith & Work, Business for the Common Good 2020, panel discussion, https://denverinstitute.org/business -for-the-common-good-2020/wholehearted-leadership/#!.

[3] Jeff Haanen, "Resetting a Career Midlife," Denver Institute for Faith & Work, September 23, 2021, https://denverinstitute.org/resetting-your-career-in-midlife/.

[4] See Terry Looper, *Sacred Pace: Four Steps to Hearing God and Aligning Yourself with His Will* (Nashville: Thomas Nelson, 2019).

[5] Fyodor Dostoevsky, *The Brothers Karamazov* (New York: Bantam Classics, 1984), 338.

[6] For an excellent treatment on how our loves and desires shape our habits and our character, see James K. A. Smith, *Desiring the Kingdom* (Grand Rapids, MI: Baker, 2010).

[7] C. S. Lewis, *The Weight of Glory, and Other Addresses* (New York: Macmillan, 1980).

[8] Here's one outstanding speech David Brooks gave on the topic: "How to Be Religious in the Public Square," *The Gathering*, October 2, 2014, https://thegath ering.com/news-posts/transcript-david-brooks-gathering-2014/.

⁹ For an excellent book on interior freedom, see Jacques Phillip, *Interior Freedom* (Strongsville, OH: Scepter, 2017).

¹⁰ This is a contemporary version of "The Principle and Foundation of the Spiritual Exercises of St. Ignatius." Quoted from David Fleming, SJ, "Praxis Resource: The Principle and Foundation," handout, Winter 2020.

¹¹ See "Spiritual Disciplines for Your Work," Denver Institute for Faith & Work, 2018, https://denverinstitute.org/spiritual-disciplines-for-your-work/.

¹² "Spiritual Disciplines for Your Work."

¹³ An outstanding book on the "with God" life is Skye Jethani, *With: Reimagining the Way You Relate to God* (Nashville: Thomas Nelson, 2011).

4. THINK THEOLOGICALLY

¹ From a personal interview on March 1, 2015.

² Charles Taylor, *A Secular Age* (Cambridge, MA: Belknap, 2018).

³ Lesslie Newbigin, *The Gospel in a Pluralist Society* (Grand Rapids, MI: Eerdmans, 1989).

⁴ I explore the story of Eventide more in depth in "Investments for the Kingdom," *Christianity Today,* November 23, 2016, http://jeffhaanen.com/2016/12/30 /investments-for-the-kingdom/.

⁵ For more information, see www.faithandinvesting.com/.

⁶ See, for instance, Michael Goheen and Craig Bartholomew, *The Drama of Scripture: Finding Our Place in the Biblical Story* (Grand Rapids, MI: Baker Academic, 2014).

⁷ See Daniel Pink, *To Sell Is Human: The Surprising Truth About Moving Others* (New York: Riverhead, 2013).

⁸ See: Brian Gray, "Selling Christianly," Business for the Common Good, Denver Institute for Faith & Work, https://denverinstitute.org/business-for-the -common-good-2020/selling-christianly/.

⁹ Al Wolters, *Creation Regained: Biblical Basics for a Reformational Worldview* (Grand Rapids, MI: Eerdmans, 2005).

¹⁰ Martin Luther King Jr., "A Tough Mind and a Tender Heart," Stanford University, August 30, 1959, https://kinginstitute.stanford.edu/king-papers/documents /draft-chapter-i-tough-mind-and-tender-heart.

¹¹ For more on this topic, see my article: Jeff Haanen, "Broader, Not Deeper," October 3, 2016, https://jeffhaanen.com/2016/10/03/broader-not-deeper/.

¹² Jeff Haanen, "What It Means to Follow Christ as a Public School Teacher," July 17, 2005, https://denverinstitute.org/what-mary-poplin-taught-us-about-being -a-christian-teacher-in-public-education-1-of-2/.

[13] Molly Worthen, "What Would Jesus Do About Inequality," *The New York Times,* December 13, 2019, www.nytimes.com/2019/12/13/opinion/sunday/christianity -inequality.html.

5. EMBRACE RELATIONSHIPS

[1] "Becoming," Faith & Co, Seattle Pacific University, August 21, 2020, YouTube video, 3:39, www.youtube.com/watch?v=wfEmU5UMSXU.

[2] Laurence Hebberd, "10 Reasons Why People Really Quit Their Jobs," *Undercover Recruiter,* https://theundercoverrecruiter.com/why-people-quit/.

[3] "Why People Quit," *Harvard Business Review,* September 2016, https://hbr .org/2016/09/why-people-quit-their-jobs.

[4] "The Top 9 Qualities of a Great Place to Work," *Top Work Places,* August 5, 2020, https://topworkplaces.com/the-top-9-qualities-of-a-great-workplace/.

[5] Edwin Friedman, *Generation to Generation* (New York: Guilford, 1985), 27.

[6] For more on this, start with Murray Bowen, *Family Therapy in Clinical Practice* (New York: Jason Aronson, 1993).

[7] Tracy originally got this quote from Jim Wilder, *Renovated* (Colorado Springs, CO: NavPress, 2020).

[8] For more information, visit: https://capablelife.me/join/.

[9] A particular thank you to Brian Gray, VP of Formation and 5280 Fellowship Director at Denver Institute for Faith & Work, for compiling this tool. Download it for free at https://denverinstitute.org/the-user-guide-to-working-with-me/.

[10] Rachel Anderson and Shannon Allen, "The Process of Biblical Conflict Resolution," May 15, 2017, www.coloradochristianmediation.com/blog/2017 /5/9/biblical-conflict-resolution.

[11] Lydia Rueger Shoaf, "Collaboration Through Conflict," Denver Institute for Faith & Work, November 8, 2021, https://denverinstitute.org/collaboration-through -conflict-stephanie-summers-on-leading-diverse-teams/.

[12] "Women in the Workplace 2021," McKinsey and Company, September 27, 2021, www.mckinsey.com/featured-insights/diversity-and-inclusion/women -in-the-workplace.

[13] "Women, Work & Calling Videos," Denver Institute for Faith & Work, March 23, 2015, https://denverinstitute.org/women-work-calling-videos/.

[14] This quote is from Jean-Pierre de Caussade, *Abandonment to Divine Providence* (Gastonia, NC: Tan, 2010).

[15] In *Working from the Inside Out,* I broadly categorize working class as those without a four-year college degree. By this measure, roughly two-thirds of American adults are working class and one-third are professionals. See, for in-stance, "An Update on Rising Mortality Rates Among White, Working-Class

Americans," *Wall Street Journal,* November 19, 2017, www.wsj.com/articles/an-update-on-the-two-americas-1510784348.

[16] Matthew B. Crawford, "Shop Class as Soulcraft," *The New Atlantis,* Summer 2016, www.thenewatlantis.com/publications/shop-class-as-soulcraft.

[17] See Robert Putnam, *Our Kids* (New York: Harper Collins, 2016), and Senator Mike Lee's Social Capital Project, www.lee.senate.gov/scp-index.

[18] Arthur Brooks, Harvard professor, social scientist, and former leader of the American Enterprise Institute, has done excellent research here. See his presentation on nonprofits, fundraising, and how people find happiness from spending money at www.hks.harvard.edu/educational-programs/executive -education/faculty/hks-executive-education-webcast-series/arthur-brooks -fundraising.

[19] Michael Simmons, "The Number 1 Predictor of Career Success According to Network Science," *Forbes,* January 15, 2015, www.forbes.com/sites/michael simmons/2015/01/15/this-is-the-1-predictor-of-career-success-according -to-network-science/?sh=16abe619e829.

[20] Donna Gray, "8 Ways to Making Your Company a Great Place to Work," *Greater Madison InBusiness,* May 29, 2013, www.ibmadison.com/8-keys-to-making -your-company-a-great-place-to-work/.

6. CREATE GOOD WORK

[1] This story first appeared at: Jeff Haanen, "Knotted Dreams," April 2, 2014, https://jeffhaanen.com/2014/04/02/knotted-dreams/.

[2] Derek Thompson, "The Religion of Workism is Making Americans Miserable," the *Atlantic,* February 24, 2019, www.theatlantic.com/ideas/archive/2019/02 /religion-workism-making-americans-miserable/583441/.

[3] See Nicholas Eberstadt, "Education and Men Without Work," *National Affairs,* Winter 2020, www.nationalaffairs.com/publications/detail/education-and -men-without-work.

[4] Jim Harter, "US Employee Engagement Data Hold Steady in First Half of 2021," Gallup, July 29, 2021, www.gallup.com/workplace/352949/employee-enga gement-holds-steady-first-half-2021.aspx.

[5] Jeff Haanen, "Where Are All the Workers? How to Revive a Wilting Workforce," *Comment,* September 1, 2022, https://comment.org/where-are-all-the-workers/.

[6] For a book on faith and retirement, see Jeff Haanen, *An Uncommon Guide to Retirement: Finding God's Purpose for the Next Season of Life* (Chicago: Moody, 2019).

[7] The CDC reported in July 2022 28.8 percent of Americans report symptoms of anxiety disorder; for 18–29-year-olds, it's a staggering 42.9 percent (www.cdc .gov/nchs/covid19/pulse/mental-health.htm).

[8] Quoted at www.hattebergwoodworks.com/.

[9] I find it interesting that in some data sets, pay is in the middle of what workers want most from their employer. However, when asked about public and political issues, fair wages and pay are often at the top for voters, as are issues about the economy in general. Harmonizing the various studies, I think that good pay is just as much about expressing a worker's worth and dignity as it is about paying the bills. For managers, pay gets employees in the door, but it's insufficient to keep them there.

[10] "Annual Survey: In an Unstable Economic Environment, Workers and Wages Are More Important Than Ever to the American Public," *Just Capital*, September 15, 2022, https://justcapital.com/reports/2022-survey-workers-and -wages-are-more-important-than-ever-to-the-american-public/.

[11] Dan Buettner, "Finding Happiness at Work," *Psychology Today*, February 21, 2011, www.psychologytoday.com/us/blog/thrive/201102/finding-happiness -work.

[12] Studs Terkel, *Working: People Talk About What They Do All Day and How They Feel About What They Do* (New York: New Press, 1972), xi.

[13] I first told a version of this story on my blog, https://jeffhaanen.com/2013/02/24 /daddy-what-if-there-were-no-stores/.

[14] Lester DeKoster, *Work: The Meaning of Your Life* (Grand Rapids, MI: Acton Institute, 1982), 2.

[15] Charles Murray, *Coming Apart: The State of White America from 1960–2010* (New York: Random House, 2012), 268, 271.

[16] John Stott, *Issues Facing Christians Today* (Grand Rapids, MI: Zondervan, 1984), 162.

[17] This story is from the film "Turning," Faith and Co., Seattle Pacific University, https://faithandco.spu.edu/film-detail/turning/.

[18] See www.craftsmanwithcharacter.org/the-craftsman-s-code.

[19] Quoted in William C. Placher, *Callings: Twenty Centuries of Christian Wisdom on Vocation* (Grand Rapids, MI: Eerdmans, 2005), 405-12.

[20] "Bikes and Baptisms: One Ukrainian Couple's Journey," Hope International, March 16, 2017, https://blog.hopeinternational.org/2017/03/16/bikes-and -baptisms/.

[21] For a more in-depth treatment of Exodus 19–20, see my sermon, "A Kingdom of Priests and a Holy Nation," Wellspring Church, July 26, 2022, https://jeffhaanen .com/2022/08/01/a-kingdom-of-priests-and-a-holy-nation-a-sermon-on -exodus-19-20/.

[22] Dan Reed, "In Search of Best-in-Class," Seed Fundraisers, June 4, 2021, www .seedfundraisers.com/post/in-search-of-best-in-class.

23 N. T. Wright, *Surprised by Hope: Rethinking Heaven, the Resurrection, and the Mission of the Church* (San Francisco: HarperOne, 2008).

24 These quotes are from a Denver Institute *Faith & Work* podcast interview, which can be found at https://denverinstitute.org/wp-content/uploads/2021/02/9 _3-Meagan-McCoy-Jones-1.pdf.

25 See my article "What's Wrong with Do What You Love," June 18, 2014, https://jeffhaanen.com/2014/06/18/whats-wrong-with-do-what-you-love/.

26 See these personal interviews we did with the late Eugene Peterson: https://jeffhaanen.com/2014/12/31/video-release-eugene-peterson-on-vocation/.

27 You can access this free download at https://denverinstitute.org/deep-rest -a-study-of-sabbath/.

28 I give more practical suggestions on how to practice sabbath in my book *An Uncommon Guide to Retirement: Finding God's Purpose for the Next Season of Life* (Chicago: Moody, 2019).

7. SERVE OTHERS SACRIFICIALLY

1 Chris Horst, "Showing Hospitality to Strangers and Spring Breakers," *Christianity Today*, May 4, 2016, www.christianitytoday.com/ct/2016/may-web-only /showing-hospitality-to-strangers-and-spring-breakers.html.

2 David Brooks, *The Road to Character* (New York: Penguin Random House, 2016).

3 See my article "Where Are All the Workers?" *Comment*, September 1, 2022, https://comment.org/where-are-all-the-workers/.

4 Dorothy Sayers, "Vocation in Work," quoted in William C. Placher, *Callings: Twenty Centuries of Christian Wisdom on Vocation* (Grand Rapids, MI: Eerdmans, 2005).

5 See "The Rationale," Ownership Works, https://ownershipworks.org/the -rationale/.

6 Tommy Beer, "Top 1% of US Households Hold 15 Times More Wealth than Bottom 50% Combined," *Forbes*, October 8, 2020, www.forbes.com/sites /tommybeer/2020/10/08/top-1-of-us-households-hold-15-times-more-wealth -than-bottom-50-combined/?sh=3067585a5179.

7 Candidly, this was my favorite interview in the book. A special thank you to Julie Stone for sharing her story, and for her beautiful revisions.

8 I highly recommend Chelsea Mize's series of three articles on the history of redlining and housing discrimination in America written for Maxwell, a fintech company based in Denver: "The Land of Unequal Opportunity (Pt. 1): A History of Redlining and Its Lasting Impact on Black Homeownership," June 20, 2020, https://himaxwell.com/resources/blog/the-land-of-unequal-opportunity

-pt-1-a-history-of-redlining; "The Land of Unequal Opportunity (Pt. 2): How Government Policy Segregated American Neighborhoods," June 25, 2020, https://himaxwell.wpengine.com/resources/blog/the-land-of-unequal-opportunity-pt-2-how-government-policy-segregated-american-neighborhoods/; "The Land of Unequal Opportunity (Pt. 3): The Path Towards an Equitable Housing Market," July 6, 2020, https://himaxwell.com/resources/blog/the-land-of-unequal-opportunity-pt-3-the-path-towards-an-equitable-housing-market.

[9] See Emmanuel Katongole and Chris Rice, *Reconciling All Things* (Downers Grove, IL: InterVarsity Press, 2008), 39-48.

[10] Brian Gray, "Saving More Than Souls," Denver Institute for Faith & Work, April 16, 2019, https://denverinstitute.org/saving-more-than-souls/.

[11] Savera is the winner for HOPE International's 2017 Thurman Award. Her story can be found at www.hopeinternational.org/learn/video-detail/2017-thurman-award-winner-savera-mutemariya.

[12] Courtney Mares, "Pope Francis: Subsidiarity Means Everyone Has a Role in Healing Society," *Catholic News Agency*, September 23, 2020, www.catholicnewsagency.com/news/45936/pope-francis-subsidiarity-means-everyone-has-a-role-in-healing-society.

[13] Steve Garber, "Vocation as Integral, Not Incidental," Washington Institute for Faith, Vocation & Culture, April 25, 2011, https://washingtoninst.org/vocation-as-integral-not-incidental/.

[14] Haanen, "Where Are All the Workers?"

[15] John Stott, *Christian Mission in the Modern World* (Downers Grove, IL: InterVarsity Press, 2008), 50.

[16] "George Washington Carver," Alabama Men's Hall of Fame, Samford University, www.samford.edu/alabama-mens-hall-of-fame/inductees/Carver.html.

[17] Quote in "Our Covenant," Maclellan Foundation, https://maclellan.net/our-covenant.

[18] For more on the story of John and Ash Marsh, see "Beauty Out of Brokenness: Marsh Collective Builds Hope," YouTube video, 9:52, www.youtube.com/watch?v=AMjeSP9z-8U.

8. HOW TO CHANGE

[1] In a sermon I gave on Exodus 19–20, I argued, "We don't become holy through effort. We become holy through association." Rather than trying to change, progress is instead made through acceptance and consenting to the Holy Spirit's transformative power in the moment. See "A Kingdom of Priests and a Holy

Nation: A Sermon on Exodus 19–20," August 1, 2022, https://jeffhaanen .com/2022/08/01/a-kingdom-of-priests-and-a-holy-nation-a-sermon-on -exodus-19-20/.

[2] Albert Y. Hsu found in his dissertation research that books can indeed change you—but the context and community in which you read the book is the key to lasting transformation. See "Transformative Reading: A Study of Transformative Learning Among Christian Emerging Adults Through Book Reading in a Digital Age," Trinity International University Proquest Dissertations Publishing, 2015, www.proquest.com/docview/1793940493.

[3] James K. A. Smith and D. Michael Lindsay, "The Hidden Curriculum of Leadership," *Comment*, May 8, 2014, https://comment.org/the-hidden -curriculum-of-leadership/.

[4] One of my favorite books on growth and change is: James K. A. Smith, *You Are What You Love: The Spiritual Power of Habit* (Grand Rapids, MI: Brazos Press, 2016).

[5] This formulation is taken from a variety of sources, including my experience. However, one of the best books I've found that touches on this comprehensive view of change is Douglas Hyde, *Dedication and Leadership* (South Bend, IN: University of Notre Dame Press, 1966).

[6] These quotations came from personal interviews I did in 2016 and 2017, published in the 2017 Denver Institute for Faith & Work annual report. I changed the names to protect the identity of my interviewees. See https://denverinstitute .org/wp-content/uploads/2018/08/2017-DIFW-Imapct-Report_rev-082718.pdf.

[7] See Philip Yancey, *The Question That Never Goes Away* (Grand Rapids, MI: Zondervan, 2013).

[8] John Ortberg, "Never Waste a Crisis," *CT Pastors,* January 1, 2011, www.christianity today.com/pastors/2011/winter/dontwastecrisis.html.

[9] Jacques Philippe, *Interior Freedom* (New York: Scepter, 2002), 29-31.

[10] I could not find the original source for this quote, but here it is as a tweet: https://twitter.com/dailykeller/status/572972318563155968.

[11] Hyde, *Dedication and Leadership*, 27.

[12] Two great secular resources here on the church, civic society, and the benefits of membership are Robert Putnam, *Our Kids* (New York: Simon & Schuster, 2016); and Timothy Carney, *Alienated America* (San Francisco: Harper Paperbacks, 2020).

[13] "The Twelve Steps," Alcoholics Anonymous, www.aa.org/sites/default/files /literature/The%20Twelve%20Steps%20of%20Alcoholics%20Anonymous%20 -%20SMF-121.pdf.

[14] For an excellent book on how stories function in ancient myths, see Joseph Campbell, *The Hero with a Thousand Faces: The Collected Works of Joseph*

Campbell (Grand Haven, MI: Brilliance Audio, 2016). For a great practical read on how to better tell stories in a professional setting, see Annette Simmons, *The Story Factor: Inspiration, Influence, and Persuasion through the Art of Storytelling* (New York: Basic Books, 2019).

[15] Quoted in Maria Popova, "William James on the Psychology of Habit," September 25, 2012, www.themarginalian.org/2012/09/25/william-james-on-habit/.

[16] Quoted in Jason Barney, "Excellence Comes by Habit: Aristotle on Moral Virtue," March 25, 2019, https://educationalrenaissance.com/2019/03/25/excellence-comes-by-habit-aristotle-on-moral-virtue/.

[17] There's lots of pseudoresearch out there on this topic. Some say it's only 58 times per day, others say 344! I took a middle number.

[18] John Maynard Keynes, *The General Theory of Employment, Interest and Money* (New York: Houghton Mifflin Harcourt, 2016).

[19] Raj Chetty, "Social Capital and Economic Mobility," Opportunity Insights: Social Capital Atlas, https://socialcapital.org/?dimension=EconomicConnectednessIndividual&dim1=EconomicConnectednessIndividual&dim2=CohesivenessClustering&dim3=CivicEngagementVolunteeringRates&geoLevel=county&selectedId=06037.

[20] *The Tree of Life*, directed and written by Terrence Malick (Los Angeles, River Road Entertainment, 2011).

9. TRANSLATING YOUR CONVICTIONS

[1] Jeff Haanen, "A Growing Charter School Planted in Rocky Soil," *Christianity Today,* August 2, 2013, www.christianitytoday.com/thisisourcity/7thcity/growing-charter-school-planted-in-rocky-soil.html.

[2] N. T. Wright, *The Challenge of Jesus: Rediscovering Who Jesus Was and Is* (Downers Grove, IL: InterVarsity Press, 1999), 187.

[3] If you want a good laugh on this topic, watch "Shoot Christians Say" on YouTube, www.youtube.com/watch?v=7Dxo0Yjno3I&t=50s.

[4] Alyson Breisch, "Reimagining Medicine: Breakout Session_04.6.16," Denver Institute for Faith & Work, April 4, 2006, https://vimeo.com/172969773.

[5] John Inazu, "The Translator" in *Uncommon Ground: Living Faithfully in a World of Difference* (Nashville: Thomas Nelson, 2021), 119, 125.

[6] For more on these four models, including examples and what I believe to be challenges with each model, see Jeff Haanen, "Faith in the Workplace: The Four Postures," Denver Institute for Faith & Work, November 17, 2017, https://denverinstitute.org/the-four-postures-toward-faith-in-the-workplace/.

[7] Lesslie Newbigin, *Truth to Tell* (Grand Rapids, MI: Eerdmans, 1991), 83-84.

[8] For another perspective on how to understand your city's (or company's) culture, see Stephen Um and Justin Buzzard, *Why Cities Matter* (Wheaton, IL: Crossway, 2013), or my review of it for *Christianity Today*, "How to Change Your Company's Culture," May 13, 2013, https://jeffhaanen.com/2013/05/13/how-to-change -your-companys-culture/.

[9] On this language of practices of engagement and abstention, see Justin Whitmel Earley, *The Common Rule* (Downers Grove, IL: InterVarsity Press, 2019).

[10] From "Faith and Work in Journalism with TGC," Denver Institute for Faith & Work, https://denverinstitute.org/wp-content/uploads/2019/03/S2E3_Faith-at -Work-in-Journalism-with-TGC.pdf.

[11] Jeff Haanen, "Designing Workplaces to Be More Human," Denver Institute for Faith & Work, 17 March 17, 2020, https://denverinstitute.org/designing -workplaces-to-be-more-human/.

[12] Emily Dickinson, "Tell All the Truth but Tell It Slant—(1263)," *Poetry Foundation*, www.poetryfoundation.org/poems/56824/tell-all-the-truth-but -tell-it-slant-1263.

10. A LIFE OF LOVE

[1] Brian Tierney, *The Idea of Natural Rights* (Grand Rapids, MI: Eerdmans, 1997).

[2] Kyle Harper, *From Shame to Sin: The Christian Transformation of Sexual Morality in Late Antiquity* (Cambridge, MA: Harvard University Press, 2013). Also see Tim Keller's first podcast in his series on *Questioning Christianity*: https://qcpodcast.gospelinlife.com.

[3] Tom Holland, *Dominion: How the Christian Revolution Remade the World* (New York: Basic Books, 2019).

[4] Tim Keller, "Nietzsche Was Right," The Gospel Coalition, September 23, 2020, www.thegospelcoalition.org/reviews/dominion-christian-revolution -tom-holland/.

[5] Francis Schaeffer, *The Mark of the Christian* (Downers Grove, IL: InterVarsity Press, 2006).

[6] On the four great temptations we face see Thomas Aquinas, *Summa Theologiae*, "Question 2: Things in Which Man's Happiness Consists," www.newadvent.org /summa/2002.htm.

[7] Bernard of Clairvaux, *Song of Songs* (Pickerington, OH: Beloved, 2014), 136.

[8] Os Guinness, *The Call: Finding and Fulfilling the Central Purpose of Your Life* (Nashville: Thomas Nelson, 2018), 161.

[9] Quoted in Margie Warrell, *Stop Playing Safe: How to Be Braver in Your Work, Leadership, and Life* (New Jersey: Wiley, 2021), 20.

Also Available

To download a free study guide for *Working from the Inside Out*, visit denverinstitute.org/working-from-the-inside-out.